Registration Methods

Registration Methods
for the Small Museum

A Guide for Historical Collections

Daniel B Reibel

American Association for State and Local History

Nashville

Publication of this book was made possible in part by funds from the sale of the Bicentennial State Histories, which were supported by the National Endowment for the Humanities.

Library of Congress Cataloguing-in-Publication Data

Reibel, Daniel B
  Registration methods for the small museum.

  Bibliography: p.
  Includes index
  1. Museum registration methods. I. American Association for State and Local History, II. Title.
AM139.R44   069'.52   78-15994
ISBN O-910050-37-6

Printed in the United States of America

Contents

archives

General Countic 25 ap 79

Preface

■ There are several problems in writing a book such as this one. First of all, there are two or three pieces of good literature on the registration field already available. That literature is quite explicit and simple and should leave little doubt in the mind of any museum manager about what must be done to have a good registration system. There is also, on the surface, a commonly agreed upon method of museum registration that is standard in the museum field. All that would seem to make it easy for anyone beginning in the field to understand completely the standard registration system and to be able to catalogue any museum collection. That appearance of ease and understanding, however, is far from the truth.

The problem with much of the literature on registration—and a pitfall I have tried to avoid in this book—is that the author presents the system that *he* uses at *his* museum and says that this is the standard of the museum field and the system you should copy. This statement does not apply to all the literature, but it is true of much of it. Every museum is different— museums have different kinds of collections, they differ in size of holdings and staff, differ in rationale of collecting, and—just differ. What I have tried to do is present the means to develop a registration system that will be as good as any and up to the current state of the art. You are going to have to do it yourself. We use a registration system at Old Economy that is similar to the one proposed in this book, but I have not suggested that our system be used by everybody. I have developed completely new registration forms for this book. I have streamlined some of the procedures we use and simplified them for a museum with a smaller staff. What I have tried to do is to develop an "ideal" system for the small museum.

There is no single national museum registration system. I collect registrars' manuals; from reading them and the available literature, and from actual observation, I can state that practically no two museums use the same system. On the surface they appear to, as you can readily see the standard *66.2.9* style of numbers all over the country, but—and it is a big *but*—none of the museums arrives at these numbers in any single manner, and none of them applies the numbers in the same way. We, as museum professionals, outwardly appear to use a system as uniform as the Dewey Decimal System—but we lack that system's consistency.

Second, the "system" is not readily apparent. I have a hobby of visiting and helping small historical societies and have been on several consulting trips for the American Association for State and Local History and accreditation visits for the American Association of Museums. I visit small and large societies wherever I go, and I know that the so-called national "system" is not understood in the field. You can go to hundreds of small historical societies and find very few administrators who know why they should have a registration system, let alone how to achieve it. The museum field itself has not resolved the difference between a *registration system,* a *documented collection,* and a *catalogue.* If you think it has, get a few of your colleagues together and ask what the difference is. You will be surprised.

This book is not an attempt to promote a standard system of registration. I do not think that is possible at this time, or even desirable. It is an attempt to help the small historical society or museum develop its own registration system—one that will conform to present museum standards and will fit its needs and ability to perform. There is no reason why the smallest volunteer-run museum cannot have as good a registration system as any. They do not need the apparatus of the large museum to have a good system. To that extent, this book is an attempt to develop a *uniform system for all small history museums.*

The third problem is that most of the good literature is written by the registrars of large art museums. The key words are *registrars* and *large.* The practices of an art museum are easily transferred to a historical museum. A registrar's business is to make sure that a museum has good registration records. That is an excellent ideal and the purpose of this book . . . but . . . the realities of the small museum do not allow for even the idea of a registrar. The one- or two-man professional staff in these museums has so many things to do that registration is just one of the *small* problems it has to solve. I have always thought that I was rated more on my ability to keep the furnace going than on the museum catalogue, and my museum is not so small. I thought that I had to develop a system that would not take too much time.

Then there is the word *small*. The American Association of Museums is considering defining a small museum as one having a budget under about $350,000, although they have not yet hit upon a final figure. To most of the people I know, that figure is a joke. In 1974, *44 percent of the museums in the country* had a budget of under $50,000, and I would guess that this has not changed much[1]. When we come to history museums, the budget picture gets even worse.

According to the same NEA study that produced the above figures, 62 percent had a budget under $50,000 and 79 percent were under $100,000. That is the picture of the small museum that was before my eyes when I was writing this book. It is unrealistic to give these museums a registration system that will fit Colonial Williamsburg, when the only full-time staff person is the curator. It is better to give them a good system they can live with and can make accurate and complete.

The fact that almost all of the literature on registration is by registrars of art museums merits comment. It is true that almost all of the techniques of registration of an art museum are transferrable to a history museum, but . . . An art museum might have a very large collection with a thousand items, but that would be a very small historical collection. From observation, I find that individual accessions in art museums tend to be small. There are often only one or two items in an accession. In the summer of 1977, I helped to accession more than seventeen hundred tools in three accessions at Old Economy, and that is

1. National Endowment for the Arts, *Museums USA* (Washington, D.C: NEA, 1974). I venture to guess that you could add about 5 percent a year to these figures and still be fairly accurate.

not the largest accession I have ever made. History museums, then, resemble science or anthropology museums in the size of their collections, but have intrinsically valuable and even artistic items in them. Art museums are much more fortunate than history museums in that they do not have as many items to keep track of, and they can have more extensive, more detailed records on each object than a history museum can afford. Reading the available literature, the tyro in the museum field is likely to feel that he does not have a catalogue unless he has eight different catalogue cards—when none at all would do. This book is an attempt to develop, for small historical museums, a useful system that will assure that every object in the museum will be registered and that the museum can account for its whole collection easily.

As can be seen from the bibliography, there is not a great deal of literature on registration available. I did not "pack" the bibliography and left out a great deal on computer programming, but there is really very little more available that would be useful for the purposes of this book.

This book is not written for registrars, although I hope they will read it and comment fairly on it. It is written for the administrator of the museum with a small staff and only one professonal. I wish every museum had a registrar. I wish Old Economy had a registrar. I was trained by a professional registrar, and some of my best friends are registrars. Many history museums do not have registrars and never will. Each museum will have to develop a system of registration that is as good as if it had the best registrar in the business. There is no reason why it cannot. I hope that all the registrars in the field will not jump on me for leaving out certain practices or for simplifying them. A registrar has time to do things that may be necessary but that may be too costly in time and personnel to be used in a small museum.

As an example, I propose a very simple system of cataloguing historic photographs—the one we used at the Detroit Historical Museum when I was there. This is not the system used by museums that have a curator of photographs or a large collection of photographs, but it will function for the small museum that has only a small collection and no curator of photographs.

As another example, I have seen a museum with about eight hundred objects in it with *six drawers of catalogue cards*—roughly, nine thousand. What a distortion of the registration process, and yet they were thinking about starting another catalogue! Surely a museum that small could make do with only one or two cards on each accession.

It is to help the small historical museum develop an adequate but feasible system that I have written this book.

Why is this book for small museums? Most of the museums in the country are small. The big ones can take care of themselves, or, at least, I think so. I know of one large state organization that has more than twenty-seven forms in its registrar's manual, and no way to receipt returned loans. Perhaps they can use this manual, too.

Acknowledgments

■ A book such as this does not develop in a vacuum. I owe a great deal to Margot Pearsall, former Curator of Social History at the Detroit Historical Museum, who taught me what a catalogue really is. Incidentally, she would disagree with some of my ideas, but she would agree that good records on every object in the museum are needed. I am also grateful to William T. Alderson, former Director of the American Association for State and Local History, for encouraging me to write this book and to Gary Gore, Director of Publications of the same organization, for all the help he gave me. The first draft was sent out to two readers whose names I do not know, and the one who could type no better than I can was very helpful. I have never met John Graham, Dorothy Dudley, and Irma B. Wilkinson, but their article and book (respectively) have been a great help to me and have been constant companions since they were published. I am also grateful to the Pennsylvania Historical and Museum Commission for allowing me the opportunities of working at Old Economy, with its completely uncatalogued collection, and of working up the system I have proposed here. Bruce Bazelon, the PH&MC Registrar, was also helpful. I have always wondered why authors always thank their wives and did not know why until I wrote this book; I now thank my wife and colleague, Patricia, for all the help she has given me.

Introduction

■ Suppose that you have a brand-new museum with a small collection and the hope and possibility of its growing. You want to do everything right; therefore, you bring in a competent curator or registrar as a consultant to advise you on collections management. The consultant will tell you what to do about conservation, storage, and record keeping, and as part of his[1] consultation with you may write a "registrar's manual"[2] for your museum. Such a manual would be a short document of ten or twelve pages, setting out all the procedures and forms necessary to have good records management or, as the familiar term in the museum field has it, "a good catalogue." A registrar's manual usually gives only the form and procedures in the registration process. I think that, for the small museum, particularly, the registrar's manual should contain policies and philosophies that affect the whole collection process of the museum. That is what I have tried to do in this book.

Registration Methods for the Small Museum is written as if we were visiting every small museum, and it has to cover many types of situations and problems. So, instead of writing an ideal registrar's manual, we are presenting a number of solutions and letting the reader pick the one that fits his situation best. In the appendix we list a number of drafts of manuals to fit several of these situations. You can take one of these manuals and arrangements as your own registrar's manual. There are several forms that you can incorporate into the manual, as well.

I have created the town and county of *Hero* for this book.

---

1. English does not have a neutral personal pronoun for indicating the third person, so I will use the standard *he*, with the understanding that it stands for the more clumsy "he or she."

2. Some professionals call this a *registration manual*.

They are, of course, right next to the town and county of *Acme*. Both towns exist, and I have been to both of them and worked on their museums' records. I have changed the names and many of the details of both places and have moved them from where they exist to Pennsylvania.

All of the examples used here are taken from my experience, no matter how farfetched some of them may sound. When I use as an example a schoolhouse at one end of the county and a mansion at the other, I am using actual examples. I have been there and have seen their collections. All but a few of the accessions cited as examples are from the records of Old Economy and do exist. Of course, the donors' names have been changed.

1

What Is a Museum Registration System?

Grandma's Attic

■ If you ever had a chance to go into grandma's attic, you've seen all of the once-valuable things there that had been used and put aside. It would have been a special thrill if you could have gone there with grandma herself; she could have told you that the old chair was *her* grandfather's—and what wonderful things he did! She could have told you about the people in the old photographs and identified all those in the picture of her wedding. All the mysterious devices you had never seen before could have been explained to you. If you have ever experienced such an adventure, you will never forget it.

But what if grandma is not there? Who would bring this material to life? The chair would be just an old chair; the photographs would show strangers; the uses of the mysterious devices would remain unknown. Grandma's wedding gown would be just an old dress carefully packed away. The objects are silent. They themselves do not speak—but grandma did. Grandma was the memory of these things. If it is not written down, that memory will be lost.[1]

The museum registration system is the memory of the museum. Long after curators and registrars have come and gone, the records of the museum will speak. In keeping the historical story straight, they are as important as the object

1. I once heard Milo M. Quaife use this analogy at a meeting in Michigan in the 1950s. The exact time and place escape my memory, but it is a good analogy to remember.

itself. A museum that fails to keep good records is failing in its primary function—some would say its only function. With good records, more than the object is preserved. With poor records, something more valuable than the object itself may be destroyed.

The person or persons in charge of a museum have been given a trust. They have been placed in charge of a collection for a little while. It is their obligation and duty to see that the collection is well cared for and that it is passed on to the next caretakers in as good condition as when they received it. Good care includes good records. Good record-keeping does not have to be difficult, nor too time-consuming, nor too costly.

There are collections of furniture, beer-bottle caps, art, matchbook covers, glass, ceramics, insulators stolen from telephone poles, seashells, animals, pornography, and so on. A museum may collect one or several of these things and more, but *not all collections are museums*. A museum has several characteristics that separate it from a mere collection. A museum is an institution that will, theoretically, last forever. A museum, no matter how private, is held in the public interest. A museum has a professional person,[2] knowledgeable about the collection, in charge of it. Private collections fail to have some or all of these characteristics.

If we had to pick just one difference between a museum and a private collection, we would say that the museum assembles its materials with the hope and intention that the collection will last forever.

The American Association of Museums defines a museum for accreditation purposes as "an organized and permanent non-profit institution, essentially educational or aesthetic in purpose, with a professional staff, which owns and utilizes tangible objects, cares for them, and exhibits them on some regular schedule."

Notice the statement that the museum *owns* and *cares for* collections. The owning of and caring for collections are the essence of the difference between being a museum and not being a museum. The records are considered an important part of

2. In volunteer-run museums, the board or the membership acts as the professional staff.

the object. Most museums that fail to be accredited fail because of the kind of care given their collections. A good percentage of such failures come about because of inadequate or incomplete records.

A museum will be considered a good museum if the staff maintains good records, but it may not be considered a museum at all if that is not done.

The museum field has developed a record-keeping system over the years that is now pretty standard—perhaps not so standard as the systems used in libraries, but consistent enough to be applied to the widely different circumstances of each museum collection. The system is actually quite simple when applied consistently. There is not much of a mystery to it, either, and there is no necessity to invent your own record-keeping system.

We already have a number of publications about museum registration systems,[3] and perhaps you wonder why we need another. Most of those now available are written by registrars—a term we will explain shortly—who work in museums with relatively large staffs. Their systems are excellent, and I would recommend them, except that they often take a lot of staff and time. But no one has ever discussed the unique problems of a history museum in a book-length treatise, for some reason, despite the fact that more than half the museums in the country are history museums. I thought a book for the small museum, written by a curator rather than a registrar, might be useful in filling that gap. The museums at which this book is aimed range from small volunteer-run organizations to museums large enough to have professional staff, but too small to have registrars.

3. The two best, in my opinion, are Dorothy H. Dudley and Irma B. Wilkinson et al., *Museum Registration Methods,* revised edition (Washington, D.C: American Association of Museums, 1968). This book is about to be revised again. It has a lot more to say about art and science museums than about history museums, but much of what is said is easily transferable. The second publication is John M. Graham II, "A Method of Museum Registration," in *Museum News Technical Supplement,* April 1964, number 2. The system Graham describes is at Colonial Williamsburg, and it is excellent, although too extensive for most museums.

Why a History Museum is Different
from an Art Museum Or Any Other Museum

A museum is a museum, but there are differences between types of museums, and these differences are often reflected in their record-keeping procedures. A history museum has two characteristics that differentiate it from other types of museum: first, the collections tend to be large. Ten or twelve thousand objects in a collection are not at all unusual, and there are many moderate-sized museums with more than a hundred thousand objects. This is also a characteristic of certain other types of museum, such as anthropological collections. However, the second differentiating characteristic of a history museum is that its collection tends to be monetarily valuable. Although no one object may be precious, the total value of the collection tends to be high. The objects also tend to have historical and aesthetic associations that make them additionally valuable out of all proportion to market value. This is a characteristic of art museums, as well.

Another characteristic of historical museums is that they often contain large collections of objects that have been poorly catalogued in the past or not catalogued at all. Such objects often have associations that are very important to the museum. Registration systems have to be flexible enough to account for these existing collections.

To allow for these characteristics, the registration systems of history museums have to be able to record a lot of data on many objects.

Definitions

It is important to understand some of the terms used in this book, so we are listing some definitions. Our definitions are not exactly those of the dictionary, but they show the way these terms are commonly understood in the museum field today:

> *Accession:* An accession is an object or a group of objects in the museum collection, from a single source.
> *Catalogue:* This is an arrangement of certain portions of the records of a museum, in categories. Usually it is all the accession information on a card in a file.

Collection: A collection is a group of objects that are associated for one reason or another. Usually the association is due to similarities in the nature of the objects, their being collected by one individual or group, or their association with one place or event. A collection may have only a few pieces in it, or it may have thousands. A museum may contain one collection, or several collections.

Curator: The term *curator* has been broadened considerably in the last few years, but for the purposes of this book the word *curator* will mean the professional person in charge of a collection. The collection may be the whole museum or only one part of it.

Documentation: Documentation is the factual information gleaned about each object in the collection. Some of this material comes with the object, and some is established by research.

Institution: For the purposes of this book, the *institution* is the organization—whether historical society, association, museum, or some larger entity—that has the ultimate ownership and authority over the collection.

Museum: For the purposes of this book, the *museum* is an institutionalized collection, the records of the collection, and the physical plant where the collection is stored and exhibited.

Object: The museum field has never come up with a generic term for the items made by man that are held in collections. A standard term is *artifact,* which is pretty good; it is a bit clumsy and does not quite fit what may be in a typical historical collection, which can include things not made by man. The word *object* is descriptive enough for our purposes here, so long as everyone understands that I am not trying to foist it off on the museum field as a generic term.

Registrar: The registrar is the person in charge of the museum's registration system. Although the practice varies widely from one museum to another, the curator usually accessions the object, and the registrar is responsible for the records after that, particularly the catalogue. In some museums, the registrar is a professional staff person, and in some, he is not. My opinion is that a registrar should be a professional staff member. In museums without a registrar, the curator(s) or the professional staff take care of the records.[4]

Registration: Registration is the whole process of creating, acquiring, and keeping records on the museum's collection and is the subject of this book.

Registration is a process of carefully organized procedures that assures the museum administrator that he can lay hands on any document or object at any stage in the registration process.

The person who is actually doing the registration or going to do it should start with the attitude that registration is just one of the problems to be solved so that some of the other problems—such as acquiring more objects for the museum, preserv-

---

4. There are rather mixed opinions in the museum field on whether the registrar or the curator should do the accessioning. In the first issue of *Registrar's Report* (May 1977), the opinion of registrars seemed to be that accessioning was one of their duties. In my opinion, the curator ought to do the accessioning of the items in his collection. This argument is somewhat academic to a museum that may not have either a curator or a registrar.

ing what you have, and interpreting the collection—can be taken care of.

Boundaries

The first thing needed in the museum as well as in the registration system is a boundary or parameter. There are certain things that should be collected and certain things that should not be. The largest parameter is detailed in the statement of purpose for the museum. If your museum has one, that is good. It should be brought out and examined to see how it fits reality. If you have a statement of purpose that reads something on this order:

> The purpose of the Hero County Historical Society is to collect and preserve historical material on Hero County and to operate a museum, to interpret this history, to own property, to publish material, to conduct educational programs, and to do anything that is worthwhile to achieve this objective.

—you are in good shape. You may collect anything that was used or may have been used in Hero County. If someone wants to give you two tons of seashells, you may turn them down, unless they are from Hero County.

On the other hand, if you have a statement of purpose that reads:

> The purpose of the Acme County Historical Society is to study, preserve and collect everything related to life on this earth, including, but not limited to, biological, artistic, scientific, and educational specimens, objects, artifacts, material and devices, both modern, ancient, and prehistoric, to conduct a museum or museums of these materials, to conduct educational programs, lectures, tours, publications and exhibits, to own property, and to do anything worthwhile to promote these ends.

—you are in trouble. No museum can function if it can potentially collect everything. There has to be a limit somewhere.

That limit is partly set by the museum's ability to preserve the object. If you are the county historical society, it does you little good to collect Japanese armor when you cannot preserve things related to your *real* purpose.

When you have a statement of purpose that is too broad, you should consult a lawyer. Perhaps there is a good reason for changing it and perhaps not. If you are legally incorporated in the state, it may be difficult or inconvenient to change the statement of purpose. If you cannot change the purpose, or do not want to, you should prepare a collection *policy* separate from the purpose.[5] The policy should be discussed with the governing body of the museum, and there should be a general agreement on what the museum is *really* trying to do and what it *can* do. The reason for the policy statement is, quite frankly, to limit the museum to what it really can do and to make sure that everyone is in agreement. A policy statement can read something like this:

> It is a policy of the Benedict Arnold Memorial Association to collect only those artifacts, publications, archival material, and other material related to the life of Benedict Arnold. The association should collect only those things of that nature that it is able to care for, preserve, store, and exhibit in a manner acceptable to the museum field at large. The curatorial committee will report from time to time all new accessions for the approval of the board, and no material will be taken into our collection until so approved. Adopted by the Board of Directors, July 4, 1776.

With such a statement as that, the museum can limit itself to what it really can do without violating its charter or constitution. Unlike a charter or constitution, a policy statement of that nature can be changed rather easily by the board. The reason for having a collections committee will be discussed below, and the person reporting could just as easily be the professional

5. Remember, the *museum's* functions may be separate from the *institution's* functions and may require a separate statement of purpose. This might be true of a university museum or the branch of a large government organization.

director or the curator. Having to report to the board gives him a ready excuse when someone offers something that is not suitable—and it helps to share with the whole board the blame for turning down a true piece of Noah's Ark, rather than having just one person responsible.

If you do not have a statement of purpose, the museum or society ought to think seriously about developing one. It is important to know what you are doing, and it is a good exercise for the board or for any governing body to think it over and decide what it is *really* trying to do.

Who Bells The Cat?

There is almost always a board or governing body *responsible* for the museum. That group must make a decision about who is actually going to do the *work*.

In a museum that has a professional staff, the decision is much easier: the professional staff does the work. The board has delegated its responsibility for the care of the museum to the professional and that person—or those persons, if the museum is big and well funded—is responsible for the records, among other things. It does not matter how large the staff is—if the curator or director is the only paid professional, he is responsible. In situations where there is more than one professional, the director may delegate his responsibility. If the museum is fortunate enough to be able to afford it, there will be a registrar, but do not get the chain of responsibility confused. The governing body is responsible and delegates its authority to the professional, who may further delegate it. If something goes wrong, it is the professional's responsibility. If the governing body allows error to continue, it is the board's responsibility. With apologies to Lewis Carroll, what I have told you three times is true.

In the case of the volunteer-run museum, the governing board not only has the responsibility, but has to do the work, as well. In that event, there is usually a person or group of persons who will willingly undertake the care of the collection. Such volunteered help may be incorporated into a collections or museum committee. The committee takes charge of the catalogue and reports to the governing body on its activities from time to time. The experience of the museum field has been that these volunteer-run museums can have very effective records. It has been my experience that, whether run by either volunteers or professionals, a museum can have the kinds of records it wants. If the governing body of the museum wants good records, it will have them, whether or not there is a professional on the staff. Unfortunately, the opposite corollary is also true.

The collections committee of the governing body offers an extra bit of continuity to the collection and can make the transition from one curator to another or from one administration to another go more easily than it would otherwise.[6] For these reasons, I feel that museums that have a governing body ought to have some committee to oversee the collections.

The Test

The Test is that the museum should be able to produce any object from its collection when any document from its registration system is picked at random. It should be able to produce all the documentation or any object picked from its collection at random.

If your museum cannot pass The Test, keep working on the problem until it can. I have seen huge museums with large professional staffs that cannot pass The Test and small volunteer-run museums that can.

Where To Start

The ideal situation is not to have a previously assembled collection at all, and you can then start from scratch. New organizations are actually very fortunate, in that respect: a new organization can develop a registrar's manual before it ever gets a single object and can have an accurate and complete system from the beginning.

Museums that already have collections may not be so lucky. If your collection has been well taken care of and you have good records, you are probably reading this book for the fun of

6. The use of collection committees is not a standard practice in the museum field, but, in my opinion, it should be.

it. If your collection has not been taken care of, and the records are in a mess, you have a problem to solve before you do anything else.

How To Approach a Previously Catalogued Collection

If your museum has a poorly catalogued collection, your first problem is to get it in shape. It is difficult to tell someone how to do that without actually seeing the collection, but there are some things that can be done with any collection.

The first is to assemble all the records you have and try to sort them out. Think of yourself as an auditor with a terrible book-keeping system that has to be straightened out, particularly as the IRS is on its way. Try to match correspondence related to your collection with objects listed in your files. If anyone was around when the mess was created, try to get him to try to straighten it out. Ask everyone who is familiar with the museum what he knows about the collection. Write letters to people who have moved. If you only sort the records you have by year, you will have made a good start.

It is a good idea to make an inventory of the museum before you move anything. Do one room at a time, making a short description of *everything* in the room. Place a temporary number on each object. That can be done with chalk, tags, or china crayon. Number the first object 1 (one), the second, 2 (two), and so on. Number the objects in the whole museum consecutively, from beginning to end, rather than start a new series of numbers in each room. Carefully make a register of the objects by number. If the collection has been numbered, these temporary numbers may be discarded when you straighten out the mess. If the collection has not been numbered or if you decide to discard the old number system, you can use these temporary numbers as your catalogue numbers. Do not leave the temporary tags on very long, especially if they are chalk. They have a way of rubbing off, and tape does not work at all. When everything has been numbered, try to match your records with the inventory.

You will end up with three classes of objects:

      a. Objects with numbers and records
      b. Objects with numbers but no records
      c. Records without a matching object

The tendency is to assume that the objects in the second category do not have any records and that the records in the third category represent stolen or missing objects. Before that assumption is made, one should try carefully to match the records with the objects. Some pretty strange descriptions creep into the files—I have seen measurements off as much as a foot, beds described as stands, cider presses described as lard presses, and so on. After you have carefully compared the records with the objects, you may have to admit that some discrepancies have crept into your records.

If possible, try to put all of one type of object together. If you have all the tables together, a description such as "one old table" may have a meaning when it is compared with the records and other tables.

Finally, never throw out old records, no matter how confused they are. Even if records are completely disorganized, someone in the future may want some information from them. All objects found in the museum when the new accession system is set up should be noted. Never discard the old numbering system. Even if you renumber everything, you should carefully note the old numbers in the new records.

The old records made sense to someone—no matter how disorganized the system may seem—and they constitute one of the primary records of the museum.

The reason old registration methods may be in a mess is often that whoever was keeping them did not complete what he set out to do and was not consistent. In museum record-keeping, if you do not want someone to curse the day you were born, you must complete what you start, and you must be consistent. It is better to do only one section of the old collection at a time, and do it well, than to try to do it all and be unable to complete what you start.

And finally, if you have a problem, reaccessioning is not always the way to solve it. You can end up with four accession numbers on each object (see sample card.) Take care of the problem and you will not have to accession it twice.

Sample Card

                                                        CAB. SHOP

No. OE77.7.33   Object: Square
  Old Numbers: 206.293
Maker: S6.350   Material: Wood
                 200.723
Date: 200.705   Origin:
                 TC1.42
Size:

      Long arm—23″ x 2 1/8″ wide x 3/8″ thick; Short arm-
          12 3/8″ x 2 1/8″ wide x 7/8″ thick.

  Description:

  SQUARE: Wood; one arm longer than the other; nail pro-
trudes from the small arm.

Penna. Historical and Museum Comm.; Div. of Historic Sites
and Prop.

Every mistake that can possibly be made has been made to register this object with six catalogue numbers. The numbers beginning with a letter represent a system that was pretty good, but we finally assigned a whole new accession number to straighten out the mess. A careful register of all the old numbers was kept, however, as they may represent relationships that no longer exist.

Volunteers and Cataloguing

There is mixed opinion among professionals in the museum field about the use of volunteers in general, and in cataloguing in particular. There is a lot of negative feeling, and volunteers tend to be used mainly in the area of interpretation and program. Volunteers can be useful in cataloguing if the professional staff will set specific and realistic goals and work with the volunteers. It is much better to say, "Let's go and catalogue the ironstone," than to say, "Go and catalogue the whole museum." Untrained volunteers can do a lot if you will line up all of one type of object and show them what characteristics to look for. Incidentally, that is a good method for professionals, as well. It is better to do twenty items well than to do a whole collection poorly.

Collectors and knowledgeable people might be willing to catalogue your collection in their area of interest. Bottle collectors might work with your bottle collection, stamp collectors with your stamps, gun collectors with your weapons, and so on. If you can tap that source of expertise, you can tap a whole community of interest that can help the museum with exhibits, publications, and collections—and they can also steer valuable items into your collection.

I, personally, find volunteers very useful, their knowledge helpful, and their enthusiasm rewarding. I would not run a museum of any size without them.

Conclusion

The first steps, then, are important. The museum should decide that it is going to have a good registration system and set out to do what is necessary to have one. It is as important to know why you are doing something as to know how to do it. It is important to stay within definite boundaries. It is even more important to be consistent and to complete each process before going on to the next step. It is important to get all the information you can on each accession and to file it where it can be found. That sounds like a lot to do, but the consequences of not doing it are worse than the job of doing it.

2

Acquisition

■ The first stage in the registration process starts with the first contact.[1] Someone may approach the museum with an item he wishes to give or sell, or the museum may approach him. Any documents created by this contact, particularly letters, bills of sale, and notes, become the first items in your accession file. Museums acquire objects by two methods, as gifts and as purchases. Items willed to you are gifts. If someone gives you money to buy an object for the collection, that is a gift.

The most important thing about these first steps in the registration process is that the museum get a document proving that the object belongs to it. You would be amazed at the number of museums that cannot prove they own their collections. The second most important characteristic of this part of the process is that the museum acquire the right to do what it wants to do with the object. The first steps that the museum takes should insure that it acquires these rights: the right to break up collections; the right to display or not to display, as the museum pleases; and the right to dispose of the object as the museum sees fit.

The rights of property may sound harsh to a prospective donor, but it is incontestably true that the donor himself would

1. See Eugene F. Kramer, "Collecting Historical Artifacts: An Aid for the Small Museum," *AASLH Technical Leaflet #6* (1970); also has information on registration.

In registering or cataloguing any collection, it is a good idea not to remove the cataloguing process very far from the objects being catalogued. In this case, the cataloguer is working in the library being catalogued.

not want to own property with any restrictions on it, and neither does the museum. Contrary to what these rights imply, the museum is under a heavy responsibility to keep anything it acquires. Museums that "churn" their collections get in trouble fast.[2] However, the museum should not be bound by an agreement to display something permanently. That would restrict it forever to one type of display. If someone gives the museum a collection of household objects, it might be expedient to store the glassware in one place, and the ceramics in another, or discard some of the collection, rather than keep it all together. Although a museum does not intend to dispose of any of its collection, there are times when it has too many of one thing and can trade or sell them and should not be restricted from doing so. It is better to acquire all these rights at the beginning and not have to worry about them later.

2. "Churning" consists of acquiring and disposing of objects rapidly.

It is fairly simple to acquire the necessary rights with things you buy, but it is not so simple with gifts.

Purchases

When the museum purchases something, it gets a bill of sale. If there has been an exchange of equal value and if this purchase is receipted or if there is some other kind of record, the museum has acquired title to the object. The bill of sale and all other documents of the transaction should be marked with the accession number of the object and placed in the accession file. The museum almost always acquires a clear title and all rights over items purchased.

If a donor gives you money to buy something, that is a gift. You still have to get a bill of sale or a receipt for the purchase, but the accession is actually a gift. Because the donor gave money, the object bought with it is much more clearly a gift than the giving of an object would be, but objects acquired this way should be treated as any other gift. Sometimes donors create funds to buy gifts, but each item bought from that fund should be acknowledged as a gift. If the item is exhibited, the label should acknowledge it as "The gift of Mrs. Deductible Item," or, in the case of a fund, "Purchased by the Faith, Hope and Charity Fund."

Even the smallest museum needs legal advice on exactly how such purchases should be handled. It is a good idea to have the museum's whole collection policy looked over by a good lawyer.

Gifts

Most small museums, and many large ones, depend on gifts to make up their collections. When someone gives an object to the museum and the transaction is "without value received," but with only good will, the museum's title to the object is not so clear as it is for a purchase. To help establish their title to gifts, museums should have all donors sign a "Transfer-of-Title Form" or "Gift Agreement Form." In the absence of any preliminary documents, that will be the first document in the museum's accession file on that particular accession. Such a form should clearly state that the donor is giving up all rights and title to the object. A statement on such a document might be:

CERTIFICATE OF GIFT

I hereby unconditionally give, donate, bestow and set over unto the Hero County Historical Society the property described on this or on the reverse side of this paper, to be used and/or disposed of by said organization in its unrestricted discretion; and for myself, my distributees and personal representatives, I waive all present or future rights in, to, or over said property, its use, or disposition.

The form for transfer of title should clearly state what is being given, show the date, and provide a place for the signatures of the donor, a witness, and a representative of the museum. With this statement, the description of the property, and all the signatures, you have a fairly good claim to the object, but title will not be absolute, and the watchful museum professional keeps that in mind. Lawyers tell me that these transfers are not worth the paper they are written on. If the donor wants the object back, you almost have to give it to him. His heirs can claim that the donor did not know what he was signing. Even with the right to reclaim his "property," however, the donor very seldom does that. In twenty-two years in the museum field, I have never seen it done. Despite that, the careful administrator never accepts *anything* unless the *actual owner* signs a transfer-of-title agreement. Appendices A and B show procedure for accepting things provisionally, pending the signing of a transfer-of-title form (shown in Appendix C) and acceptance, but never, never, NEVER accept anything without having this gift agreement signed.

Laws governing title to museum acquisitions vary widely from state to state, and local laws may enter into the question. The museum's charter or constitution may affect your ability to acquire property. Every museum should have a lawyer to help write the gift agreement. It is a good idea to have on the governing board a lawyer who exercises some sort of legal supervision in all museum affairs, including this. As conditions change, the gift agreement may need to be rewritten from time to time.

With bequests to the museum, the executor or the lawyer handling the estate will usually provide some legal document, such as a copy of the will, or something similar, that will establish the museum's title to the object. In some cases, he may produce only a letter stating that he is executing the will and has the power to transfer the property to the museum. These documents are usually sufficient to establish title to the object and you will not need a certificate-of-gift form signed, but every time that comes up, you should clear it with your lawyer.

Occasionally, you will be bequeathed items that have restrictions on them. These restrictions might include the way the gift is to be acknowledged ("in Memory of B. Knott Forgotten"), but they might also include objects you do not want or restrictions on the bequest, such as requiring that it be kept together in a collection or permanently exhibited. Each incident must be handled individually, but the institution must be careful not to place itself in the position of not being able to break up a collection or of always having to exhibit some particular object. You may have to keep bequests permanently, unlike other portions of your collection, unless you return them to the heirs. In those instances, a good lawyer is your best aid.

Sometimes heirs to an estate will give you items in memory of the deceased. These are not bequests from the estate, but are gifts from the heirs, and have to be treated as any other gift.

Museums also acquire items by law. Objects are turned over to the museum by the normal legislative process. One example would be of all the Hero County Civil War battle flags being turned over to the Hero County Historical Society by action of the county commissioners. It would be a good idea—mandatory, as a matter of fact—to get a signed letter of transmittal for such a gift. Some objects, such as archives, are turned over automatically by law. A receipt may be enough here, but you can never get too much legal advice, so ask your lawyer.

At this point, whether it was a purchase or a gift, the object is now in possession of the museum, and you have title to it. If you do not, go back to Go and start again.

Acknowledgment of Gifts

It is an excellent idea to acknowledge all gifts, both privately and publicly. There are several ways to do that. Many organizations have a printed form that they send to the donor to acknowledge a gift. That is adequate, but I prefer a personal letter. A gift is a declaration of faith in the museum and deserves more than a form letter. It takes very little effort to make each one personal:

HERO COUNTY HISTORICAL SOCIETY
Mansion on the Hill
Hero, Pennsylvania 15000

March 29, 1977

Mrs. B. Generous Donor
Gratitude Way
Hero, Pennsylvania 15000

Dear Mrs. Donor:

We wish to thank you for the gift of your collection of two thousand commemorative teaspoons. We are going to call this "The Donor Collection." We have a large number of topical collections in our museum, and this greatly improves the scope and size of our holdings. We are planning an exhibit of your teaspoons in our "Collector's Corner" and in our "New Accessions" case in May and September, respectively.

I want to thank you on behalf of the museum and the Board of Directors of the Hero County Historical Society.

Sincerely yours,

I. M. Acquisitive, Chairman
Museum Committee
Hero County Historical Society

IMA/bt
77.33

The person who receives this letter will know you really appreciate the gift. Notice the accession number at the lower left. A carbon copy of this letter and of Mrs. Donor's letter of inquiry asking the museum if it wants the collection are placed in the accession file. All of these documents may help to prove the museum's claim to title in the future if the heirs should claim that auntie did not know what she was doing when she gave away the spoons.

A good place to acknowledge a gift publicly is in your newsletter. It will give good publicity among the people most interested in the museum and will encourage them to give, also. Another place is a new accessions exhibit in some good corner of the museum. This will be seen by the casual visitor. These little gestures mean a lot. Every time an object is exhibited, it should have the donor's name on the label: "Gift of Mrs. B. Generous Donor." This is important, and the donor, his family, and friends will receive a great deal of satisfaction from seeing the name on the label. If the name is left off, the donor and potential donors quite rightfully might think you do not care.

Board Action

The museum board or governing body is responsible for the museum that owns the collection and, in a sense, the board itself can be said to own the collection. It is a good idea to have it formally approve any gift to the museum. This approval can be in the form of a report submitted periodically. Annually is often enough. This approval procedure protects the museum from the excesses of enthusiastic curators and donors and keeps the board informed. Circumstances vary widely, so I have not recommended that this be a mandatory part of the registrar's manual. However, any group setting a collections policy ought to have a very good reason for not accounting to the governing body.

If board approval is needed before the object can finally be a part of the collection, the acceptance of the gift should be made provisional on such acceptance. It should be made clear that the museum does not expect any problems—in fact, it is wise to mention, in passing, that the board must approve. If the museum does not want an object and the donor will not accept a refusal, the prospective donor should be informed that the museum cannot accept the object until the board meets. The acceptance of the collections report should be a routine thing similar to the secretary's reading of the minutes. The report merely reminds board members that the board has the final responsibility.

What Not To Do and When Not To Do It

We repeat ourselves, here, on several things that we've already suggested should not be done in acquiring an object. Once more, with feeling:

1. *Do not accept a gift without a transfer of title or buy an object without a bill of sale.*
2. *Be very careful about accepting a gift that has restrictions on its use.*

It is not a good idea to accept an object on loan pending its donation as a gift. Flexibility must be exercised, here, as sometimes the potential donor does not have title just yet and is willing for the museum to have possession of the object until he is free to give it. These types of "gifts" should not be accepted without a very clear understanding of just what is to take place and when. I would not recommend keeping such objects more than a year, but if you must, make the loan for a year, renewable year-to-year. The "donor" can come back at any time and reclaim his property, and the museum merely acts as free storage for it.

The major mistake that a museum can make in the acquisition process is to put a "valuation" on the object for tax purposes. It is considered unethical to "buy" a donation with a high or inflated evaluation. It is illegal, too. The museum can protect itself by making it part of the collection policy or the registrar's manual not to make evaluations. It is the donor's responsibility to get the evaluation. You should be more than willing to cooperate with him on getting a professional evaluation and by making the object available to the evaluator. As part of the gift, the donor may want the museum to pay for the evaluation, which is the same, actually, as the museum's making the evaluation, and it should not be done. You may lose an item every now and then because of refusal to do this, but you will keep your integrity.

On the other hand, the value is often part of the description. You may have two china plates, one of which is worth five hundred dollars, while the other is worth fifty cents. Another example would be an object associated with a famous person. The association gives it a value beyond its value as an artifact. You might have a cider press made in Hero County that would be worth fifty dollars, anywhere else, but here is worth two hundred because of local interest. If you insure your collection, the insurance value may be an evaluation, too. These are "book" values and not necessarily the real ones. You might inform the donor of this "book" value, but I strongly recommend that you do not. At one time we informed donors of the book value, and the IRS advised us that that was proper; however, we no longer give donors "book value" figures, as we feel we are getting into an area, there, where we do not belong.

A museum also has to be very careful about giving "life tenure" to the donor on objects or collections. This is particularly true when a tax deduction is involved. The donor usually cannot claim tax deductions unless the property has been transfered to and is in the possession of the museum. You also may have trouble getting your property away from the heirs. Museums are usually not in a position to engage in long and expensive law suits.

On the other hand, if the object will be a valuable addition to your collection and the owner does not want to let go of it just yet, giving life tenure may be a way to acquire something. In such instances, the owner may be more worried about his estate than about his current taxes. Life tenure and long-term loan arrangements are good things to stay out of, but they are not always bad. Before entering into such an arrangement, get good legal advice.

Ethics Code

A legal friend once advised me never to do anything, no matter how innocent, that I would not mind discussing in open court. That is a good rule to follow. Ethics codes usually want people to avoid even the appearance of impropriety, and the museum collection is one area where that is a good practice.

The museum field itself has not evolved an ethics code to fit all museums, nor is this book involved in that question.[3] If the museum board feels it must have an ethics code, members should consider several factors unique to the history museum field.

It is not a good idea at all for the curator or the professional staff to be involved in the actual business of privately buying and selling in the same area in which the museum's collection falls. A good curator will, as a matter of course, be knowledgeable about areas similar to that of the museum's collection and may privately own objects that could be in its collection. He will buy and sell from time to time. He should inform his board if he has substantial holdings. If an item that should be added to the museum's collection is offered for sale to the curator, he should offer the museum first refusal. If the curator sells some of his own collection, he should offer it to the museum first.

A knowledge of the marketplace is desirable in a curator. Almost all great collections have been built by a collaboration between the curator and a dealer or dealers. On the other hand, it is an undesirable thing for the curator to operate an antiques shop on the side or to be a partner in one (silent or otherwise), or to have any similar conflict of interest. I personally do not collect in the same area as any museum at which I work, but it is pertinent to remember that for other curators to do so may be desirable. If there is a potential conflict, the board should set up a mechanism so that neither party is injured, but under which both can operate.

3. *Museum Ethics: A Report to the American Association of Museums* . . . *1978* (Washington, D.C.: American Association of Museums, 1978). See particularly pp. 18-19.

Properties Are Not Collections

We should be aware of the difference between items acquired for the collection—which should include only items that belong in the collection and are to be kept there—and other museum properties such as exhibit cases, office equipment, and similar items. The latter are properties used in the operation of the museum and should not be considered collections. If your museum does collect similar things, it should consider them *properties* until you are willing to stop using them and start preserving them. People will often give you properties, but properties should be acknowledged in a different fashion. A simple letter of thanks and perhaps a public acknowledgement will do, even though you may need the stencil-cutter much more than you need a china bowl.

The Accession File

At this point, you have a group of documents associated with the collection and a file. Some museums have a file on each accession and some have one for the year. The kind you have will depend on the number of documents you acquire and on your ability to store them. In any case, the accession number should be written in soft (no. 2) pencil on each document, so that it is associated with the object. An accession file will continue to grow as letters and other documents continue to come in, years after the file is set up. This is a permanent record of the museum and should be kept in a fire-resistant file cabinet, if you can afford one. It is not a bad idea to microfilm this file periodically. (See chapter 6, on documentation.)

To review: The first step in the registration process is the acquisition of the object. The museum must make sure that it actually acquires title to the object, that there are no restrictions on the museum's use of the object, and that all the information about the object is recorded.

3

The Mysterious Accession Number

■ One of the fascinating things about museum registration systems is the accession number. Every museum one visits has these mysterious little red—or white or green or black, or

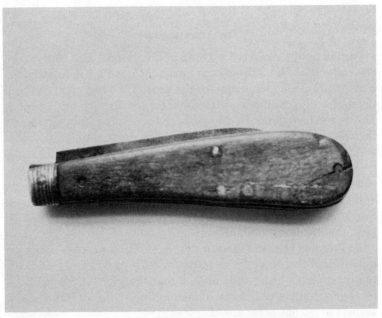

A pocket knife with its accession number. The number has been painted on a layer of nail polish. The paint is the type used for model airplanes, but could easily be sign painters' enamel. Another layer of nail polish is put on top to protect the number. The number has two characteristics: it is fixed to the object very firmly but can be removed if necessary without damaging the object.

whatever—numbers painted on every object. As a matter of fact, there had better be a little number applied to every object, or there is something wrong with the system.

I am writing this book in the hope that it may be useful to many museums, under many circumstances. If you will stay with me, I am going to use the methods of numbering objects to try to explain the rationale of museum registration systems and the various choices offered. It might be best to propose just one system and say "this is it," but museums vary, and administrators should be aware of alternatives.

A book may contain any portion of the world's knowledge,

It is a good idea to store similar objects together. It simplifies cataloguing. While you are placing locations, it is about as easy to identify a location by the shelf as it is by the room.

but, within reasonable limits, all books are about the same size and shape. In a library all the books except a few oversized and ephemeral pieces can be placed on shelves. In a library with open stacks, these shelved books become the displays, the storage, and the use-items, all at once. Not only that, the books can be shelved in any order the librarian finds meaningful. In the United States, most libraries use a registration system that categorizes the books by subject. They can be placed on the shelves in consecutive catalogue number order and be neatly classified by subject and by author inside each subject. In a library with open shelves, readers can look up one book on a subject and find almost the entire holding of the library on that subject shelved right along with that one book.

It would be wonderful if such a system would work in a museum. Alas, it will not. Some museum objects are large, and some are small; some are heavy, and some are light; some are valuable, and some are not. Good storage practice in a museum usually requires that all the objects of one class be stored together, but some objects are displayed and some are used in demonstrations or for study. One might, at one time, get an automobile and the costume of the person who rode in it. For these reasons and many more, museums find it expedient to assign numbers to objects as they come in and do their classifying in the catalogue.

We are going to start with a simple sequential system and try to show why museums use one system over another and why one system varies from another. Just because the most complex system is a later development and more refined than simpler systems, it does not necessarily follow that the more complex system is best for your museum. The best policy is to keep an open mind and adopt what you think will work best.

The Accession Number

The accession number is a handle on which you hang your whole system. It is a registration number and can tell a lot about the accession. Each number is unique to the object it is applied to. There should never be any question about the number. Any system used should insure that only one number be used for each object and that number is issued only once. This is best accomplished if only one person issues numbers and if they are issued from only one source.

The easiest system to use is a sequential system. Indeed, all systems in use today are sequential systems in one form or another. The number serves two purposes: it gives the source of the accession, and it serves as a catalogue number. Even the Single-Number System proposed here does these two things. The accession number can do more, however.

The Single-Number System

The easiest system to use is a system that has only one number. The first object in the collection is numbered "1" (one), the second "2" (two), and the 487th, "487," *seriatim*. Nothing could be simpler than that. The Single-Number System has many advantages for the small museum, as it can be easily understood by successive registrars and can give the size of the collection. In volunteer-run organizations, there is often a period between registrars. Anyone can pick up the Single-Number System in a few minutes. This system may not look right to anyone who has seen other museum registration methods, but a small museum with a small collection and a small staff may find it more useful than others. It can be adapted to approach the more "advanced" systems rather easily. (Just because a system has more numbers, it is not necessarily more advanced.) The Single-Number System is used by the largest collection in the country, the Smithsonian.

There are some disadvantages. In an accession comprising more than one object, there will not be any particular number assigned to the whole accession. There is also a tendency to confuse 7 with 1 and 6 with 9 and 4 with 5. The numbers all look different upside down. There may be a time when accessions need to be accounted for by the year or by some other period, and in such instances the lack of calendar divisions in the Single-Number System can be somewhat confusing.

The Two-Number System

To solve some of these problems, museums often use what I am going to call a *control number*. The second number arranges the accessions into blocks. When there is a problem, one has to search only the block rather than the whole accession record. Accounting for all the accessions in a single year or in any other period of time is simplified.

The most commonly used control number is the year. Usually that is the year in which the accession was made. In 1977, the number used would be *77;* in 1978, it would be *78,* and so on. The accession numbers would look like this: *77.25* or *26.77.*

Most history museums using this system use the former number in preference to the latter. It is a rather arbitrary choice, but if you plan to improve your system, I think you will find that placing the year first is simpler.[1]

With this system, you are using a number that has both a control, the year, and an accession number. The whole may be considered a catalogue number, as well. By looking at the number, you can tell something about the accession. A number such as *77.26* tells you that the object carrying it was the twenty-sixth item accessioned in 1977. Although that may not be much, it is telling you a lot more than a number such as *487.*

Sometimes there is a good reason for using some control other than the year. You may have to account for accessions by fiscal year. I would heartily recommend that any museum that wants to use a control other than the year get lots of good outside advice from *real* experts.

The Three-Number System

The big problem with the two systems outlined above is that they do not identify the source of the accession. Sometimes you are looking for a donor and the One- and Two-Number systems do not identify him by number. Museums that have a lot of accessions in the year, a number of people accessioning, and a large collection, use a third number that we will call a *catalogue number.* If you get twenty-two items in the twenty-sixth accession for the year 1977, the last item in that accession would have a number like this: *77.26.22.*

---

1. Museums that receive very few objects and only one object in an accession often use the system with the year last—that is, *26.77*—as they are more interested in the accession number than in the control.

A glance at that number will tell you that this is the twenty-second item in the twenty-sixth accession in 1977. It also tells you that all 77.26 items came from the same source. If you are looking for specific information about your collection, you can search for the year, the accession number, or the catalogue number.

Some museums write the number 22.26.77. If the most important information you need is the catalogue number, that system has value. Otherwise, I recommend placing the control number first.

The museum field has developed these systems over a number of years and has refined them to the point where they are simple and explicit. It isn't necessary to reinvent the wheel with your own system unless there is some overriding compulsion for it, and then it's wise to get expert advice before you do.

How to Evaluate Your Particular Need

Each system has something to recommend it over the others, and any choice made will be arbitrary. It is logical to start with the simplest system that fits your needs. As those needs change, one system can be adapted to the others quite easily.

Without placing a qualitative value on any system, I recommend using the One-Number System in a small volunteer-run museum. This system is self-explanatory.

I should use the Three-Number System in all other situations, with the exception listed below. The Three-Number System is pretty much the standard of the museum field at present and does identify the source with a particular number.

I should use the Two-Number System in a museum that receives only one object at a time from a limited number of sources and has a relatively static collection. An example would be a museum of historic paintings that has 125 items in its collection, mostly acquired from separate sources.

Always, it is essential to keep in mind what you are really trying to do, who is going to do the work, and what the size of the collection is. A big collection to some may be a small collection to others.

You Think We Are through with Numbers, but We Are Not

Often a museum will establish a registration system when it already has a collection. As often as not, one or more systems will have been used for such a collection, unsuccessfully. Before any new system is adopted, what has gone on before should be carefully examined to make sure that a good system is not being destroyed. The previously used system may have been poorly or inconsistently applied, but it may be acceptable otherwise. A common mistake among amateurs is to replace one bad system with another. No matter how weird the old system may look, on the surface, it may work better, with correction and refining, than a new and untried one. You can also end one system and start another, which is commonly done. No matter what you do, you are still going to have to correct the old system originally used on the collection—or at least make it consistent with the new one you are establishing. Remember, no matter how inadequate it may seem, the old system was rational to someone. Try to figure out his reasoning. I have seen a collection catalogued with Dewey Decimal numbers—and you know what? It wasn't bad, though it was clumsy.

How To Handle A Collection That Has Not Been Accessioned

If you have a collection that has not been registered before, incorporating it into your holdings is quite simple. You simply assign an artificial control number. This is usually an artificial year. As an example, if you start your new system in 1977, all the items already in your collection would have the control number 76 (or before 1977). The first object you pick up from your existing collection you number 76.1, the second, 76.2, and so on. Any new material coming into the museum would be numbered 77 (in the year 1977)—the first accession, 77.1, the second, 77.2, seriatim. Museums are supposed to last forever. In the year 2020, the people following you might find two numbers: 76.39, Spoon, or 77.26.1, Dish. They would know immediately that the spoon was in the museum before the newer registration system was adopted, and its documentation is suspect. They would know that the dish is from the new system and should have better records. This system will work, with both systems having controls—that is, with the Two-Number and Three-Number systems. If you are using the Three-Number System, you will find it is easier to use the Two-Number System with the old collection, unless you find a large group of objects that you know are associated with each other.

If you are using the One-Number System, or the system without controls, there are several methods you can use to account for items already in your collection. The best way to account for the original collection with the Single-Number System is to count all the objects. That will work, of course, only in very small collections; or, if you have inventories, it will work with large collections. When you know the size of the collection, you assign a portion of your available numbers[2] to these items. If you find two hundred objects in your collection, you assign the first three hundred numbers to the "unknown." The extra numbers are to allow for errors in counting or for items you missed.

You might assign a letter at the front of the number, such as "N" (for "no number"), so that the twenty-sixth item found in the museum will be N26. Even with the Single-Number System, you might use a control with these objects. That would mean that, in the future, any number found with a control number would be from the portion of the collection found in the museum when the registration process started. You would have numbers that look like this: *77.26, Spoon,* and *26, Dish,* in which *77.26* is from the old collection and *26* is from the new. An explanation of what has been done and why should be placed in the front of the accession book. That will explain the system in case the registrar's manual is lost or forgotten.

Whatever system you use, be consistent.

Collection Numbers

Museums are made up of separate collections, and there is sometimes a good reason for identifying each collection as distinct from the others. That might happen when a large un-

---

2. Which is, of course, infinity.

cataloged collection is received from another museum or predecessor organization. Or the museum might have two or more widely separated operations that should be kept apart: you might have a schoolhouse at one end of the county and a mansion at the other and want to keep the two collections separate, at least on paper. In that event, you would assign the letter S for the schoolhouse and M for the mansion. A collection number would look like this:

S26	or	S77.26	or	S77.26.1
M26	or	M77.26	or	M77.26.1

If you used numerals for a collection number, they would look something like this:

1.26	or	1.77.26	or	1.77.26.1
2.26	or	2.77.26	or	2.77.26.1

With such a system, you can easily identify items by their assignment to either collection. The possibilities for confusion are endless. The only reason for having a collection number is for ready identification of collections.[3] I would not recommend establishing a collection number unless you have a compelling reason for doing it and a staff to administer it. Before taking that step, consider assigning readily recognizable accession numbers for each collection, or other alternatives.

Pre-Existing Collections

The reason for discussing a collection number at all in a book aimed at small museums is that the administrator will often find collections of known provenance already established in the collection. A typical example is a museum that contains the collection from its predecessor organization (a D.A.R. museum, for instance), with the requirement to keep the predecessor's ob-

3. A good example of the need for a collection number is the system used by the Pennsylvania Historical and Museum Commission, which has sixty sites across the state and about fifty-five professional people capable of making an accession. To avoid confusion, each site is assigned a two-letter code (Old Economy is OE), and anyone can figure where the accession originated. There is a master accession number that is kept by the registrar, but this is not placed on the object.

jects as a separate collection. Someone gave the museum a collection of birds in 1910 and a log cabin with its contents in 1933, and the museum acquired a defunct school system museum in 1956, also with the understanding that the collections be kept distinct. If you think this is exaggerated, I am describing a collection I had to administer once (with the exception of the log cabin), along with thirty years of poor record-keeping.

In these cases, it is better to assign a control number, rather than a collection number. All things considered, a separate control number is a collection number. Using the examples given above, you would assign a separate control for each situation. Then, if you found these numbers on objects, you would know quite a bit about them:

> 09.26 (from the D.A.R. museum founded in 1909)
> 10.26 (from the bird collection given in 1910)
> 33.26 (from the log cabin given to the museum in 1933)
> 56.26 (from the defunct school system given in 1956)
> 76.26 (from the museum collection before the new registration system was started in 1977, but not including any of the known collections)
> 77.26 (from the museum collection after the new registration system was adopted)

This system will work best with the Two- and Three-Number systems, which may be good reason for adopting one or the other if your museum contains other collections. An adaptation of this procedure could be used with the One-Number System, perhaps using the controls for the earlier collection and the One-Number System for the new accessions.

It was a relatively common practice for museums that were started in the nineteenth and early twentieth centuries to have accession ledgers. The objects were entered into them by date of acquisition. There often would not be a number assigned. In these cases, it is best to use the Two- or Three-Number System. Since you know the year received and the order inside the year,

Registration, Step by Step:
Chain of Actions in the Registration of a Single Accession

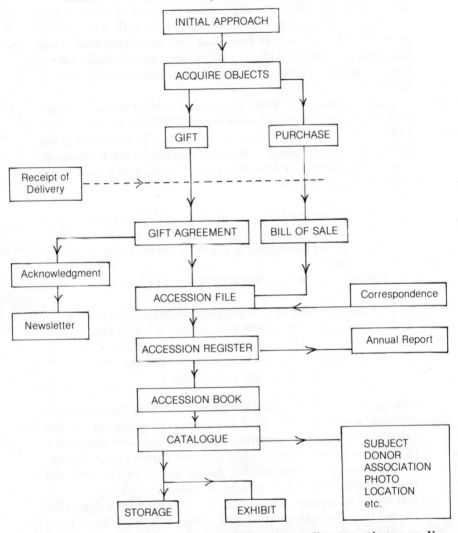

Although this may seem to be a lot of actions, there really are not that many. You will notice that each step follows the one before. The sequence is logical and no step can be started until the one before it is completed. It would be a good idea to make up such a chart for your registration system and post it.

In this chart, the actions of the Registrar's Manual in Appendix B are shown. The simpler manual in Appendix A would have fewer steps. I have placed the Receipt-of-Delivery Form in the process after the acquisition to show where it fits, although I do not recommend that all museums use it. I have also shown more catalogues than I feel a small museum needs, although certain of them might need even more than this number.

it is easy to assign a control (which would be the actual year received) and an accession number (which would be the number of the object in the order accessioned for that year). Numbers could be written on the objects as they are found. If these ledgers are printed on poor paper, as they often are, it would be best to make a working copy. You are probably going to have to use numerals indicating the whole year (i.e., 1872) as a control in these cases (see below).

This is preparing you for the circumstance in which there have been nine different registrars using nine different systems, some good and some bad, and none consistent. I have seen objects in my collection with six different accession numbers in an area I could cover with my thumb—and none of them related to the records. If this is your circumstance, take your time. Before you completely discard the old system, remember that it was once logical to someone, and the number may indicate a relationship that is important. If you have a system like this, it may be best to call in an expert and see if a portion of the old system or systems can be salvaged. Even if you discard the old system, the old numbers should be indicated in your catalogue and the old records should be retained. You may want those old numbers and records some day. In my particular instance, I found that one of the five systems in use was not bad and retained it for the items that actually bore numbers and used the Three-Number System for the rest.

Objects from unknown sources suddenly turn up in even the best-run collections. Museums using the Three-Number System will find that there is an easy way to keep track of these "unknowns." If the first accession number in each year—that is, 1 (one), is assigned to these unknown numbers every year, they will be positively identified. With that arrangement, an object with a number such as 79.1.37 would be understood to have no known source, and one with a number such as 79.2.1 would be of a known source.

What To Do About The Year 2000

All of our neat little numbering systems will get in trouble when the year 2000 arrives. It is actually quite simple—the centennial year is added to the control number. The accession numbers in the year 2000 will look like this:

000.26 or $000.26.1$

In 2007, they would look like this:

007.26 or $007.26.1$

And in 2037, they would look like this:

037.26 or $037.26.1$

You have to think in terms of collections lasting forever. It is not good enough to start using the same controls over again. Ultimately, in a hundred years, confusion will result. When the year 3000 rolls around, a fourth control unit would have to be added.

Some collections go back to the nineteenth century, or even the eighteenth. In these instances, the museum will have to use a four-digit number or numerals for the complete year date. Objects from the nineteenth century would be identified with the control 19, those from the twentieth century with the number 20, and so on. An object with the number $1876.26.3$ would be from the nineteenth century, one with the number $1976.26.1$ would be from the twentieth, and $2076.26.1$, from the twenty-first century. This is a simple decision to make, once you know your collection, but it is important to stick to the decision, once made, and to be consistent.

This is not a problem with the single sequential number, and people using that system will come in to work on January 2, 2000, with a slight hangover and just take up where they left off.

What Not To Do and When Not To Do It

Never, never, NEVER assign two accession numbers to the same object. Even the most intelligent and best-organized of us sometimes make a mistake and place an object in the wrong accession or fail to accession it properly. If you are working in the same year as the offending accession, you can just alter your records and change the number on the object. However, it is a very poor policy to do that in records for previous years. If you find a mis-accessioned object, make some notes to that effect in your records and catalogue, but leave the accession number alone. Once a number is permanently assigned and the accession made, the number should be considered as sacred as the Bible. That is why it is important to have a logical sequence of actions consistently followed.

Never fail to place the accession number on the object. If you do and if you do not keep an accurate register, you are creating a mess that may take years to clean up.

There seems to be some overwhelming compulsion on the part of registrars to place letters in a perfectly good numbering system for no reason that I can see. A typical example is the accessioning of a coffeepot, "a" and its lid, "b," thus:

77.26.12a   Coffeepot
77.26.12b   Lid for coffeepot
          or
77.36.12a   Left shoe of a pair
77.36.12b   Right shoe from the pair

That is belaboring the obvious. If in your description you mention that the coffeepot has a lid and you find a lid with the number 77.26.12 on it, you hardly need the letter b to tell you that this is a lid, and a quick glance at the records will tell you there should be a pot with the lid. If you need excessive numbers and letters to identify an object, you are probably doing too much. Three sets of numbers, such as 77.26.104, are enough to do just about everything any museum might require.[4]

On the other hand, it might be a good idea to mark pairs or sets of exactly identical objects with letter designations such as a and b. An example would be a pair of stockings. I would confine this practice to objects that will be permanently associated together. A set of dining room chairs, for example, might get separated, and each should have a separate number, while the pair of stockings, used as the example above, would not be separated and could be marked with one accession number and a letter designation, to separate them. It is important to have a

4. A lot of museums disagree with me on this point.

Archives are a very important part of a museum, but cataloguing them differs from cataloguing the objects in the collection.

consistent policy on this aspect of accessioning.

Unless you have a highly specialized collection, assigning numbers by categories is unworkable—for example, *T* for tool, *H* for household, *F* for furniture, and so on. These devices break down almost as soon as they are established. Categorization is the function of the catalogue, not the accession system.

Catalogue Numbers

Some museums have a catalogue number separate from their accession number. I have never quite understood the reasoning behind that, but such a practice is completely unnecessary for the small museum. Your accession number, whether it is the One-, Two-, or Three-Number system, will function quite as well as a catalogue number.

The Final Word on Numbers

The final word on assigning numbers is that the systems outlined above are mainly used for objects in a history museum, although they will work for objects in other collections. There are already perfectly good systems available for books, archives, some types of anthropological specimens, and for several other categories. The systems discussed here should not be used in those situations without consulting an authority.

I am sorry that we have spent so much time on numbers, but an understanding of the alternatives helps to understand quite a bit about the accessioning process. It also helps to make clear that the number can indicate more about the object than its place in the sequence. The main thing needed is to evaluate your museum's needs carefully and pick the simplest system that fits them.

4

Accessioning

■ The second stage of the registration is the *accession*, or the accessioning process. Among original meanings of the word were the act of establishing a right or claim to something or an increase by something added—essentially its meaning today. The word was once a noun, but now is also a verb and may be used as participle or gerund. The way the word is now used by museums (as a verb) means the process of taking an object or objects into the collection. We often speak of an *accession* when we mean an object or group of objects taken into our collection. We speak of *accessioning*, which describes the process of registration, when we place a description in our records, assign a number, and create other records. Accessioning is the key to a good registration system. Without any other records, a whole registration system can be created from good accession records alone. If one does nothing else, one ought to make sure that this particular stage in the registration process is performed well. It does not have to be complex or time-consuming, but, if not done properly, accessioning is the point at which everything starts to go wrong.

An *accession is an object or group of objects received from a single source at one time.* If three objects from one donor are received at one time, that is a single accession. If 486 objects from a single source are received at one time, that is an accession. If one object from a single source is received, that is an accession. On the other hand, an item in the collection is also called an *accession* even when it is part of a larger accession. All this would be somewhat irrelevant, except that people often confuse their accession records with their catalogue. It is possible to have a good museum without a catalogue and be as happy as a clam, but you may not be considered a museum at all unless you have good accession records.

When you accession, you do three things: 1. you assign to an object a number that is unique to that object; 2. you describe the object; 3. you establish the provenance or history. None of these is particularly complicated, time-consuming, or difficult.

Descriptions While Standing on One Foot

The basic part of the registration of an accession is the description of the object. Descriptions should be simple and short, but complete enough to be used in court. If you follow the journalistic "who, what, where, when, and why," you have a fairly complete description. It is best to establish a certain order to follow so that you give a complete description every time. Using a simple table as an example, you might cover the essential points in the description in this order:

What	Table
Material	Walnut
Characteristics	Four tapered legs; taper on inside; outside batten; flush drawer, brass pulls; stained and varnished; Hepplewhite style.
Condition	Excellent
Provenance	New England, early nineteenth century; in Jones family since 1862
Other Information	Donor said table was used when Hero town charter written; exhibited NYFS Museum, in NY Cabinetmaker's Show, 1924
Size	64 1/2" x 29 1/2" x 38 3/4"

Written as a description, it might look like this:

> 77.26.1 *Table:* walnut; Hepplewhite style; four tapered legs, taper on inside; loose top with outside batten set in dovetails; flush drawer with original brass pulls; stained and varnished; excellent condition; New England, early nineteenth century, perhaps local in manufacture; in donor's family since at least 1862, when mentioned in will; donor says this was the table on which grandfather (William Jones, 1822-1908) wrote Hero town charter in 1858; exhibited in "The New England Country Cabinetmaker," NYFS, 1924, see catalog in Acc/file; see also probate of Adam Jones's will, 2/9/1862, Courthouse. 66 1/2" long x 29 1/2" high x 38 3/4" deep.

Usually, one develops a sort of laconic style, leaving out all unnecessary wording. If subjectless or verbless statements separated by semicolons are used, the descriptions are shorter. These descriptions do not have to have any literary merit—they just have to be complete enough to identify that particular table. It would be lovely if the descriptions would evoke an accurate picture of the object in the reader's mind, especially if he were unfamiliar with the object. The writing of descriptions is not an exercise in creative writing, however—all one is trying to do is to describe what is unique to the object. Short, succinct descriptions are best. The reader of a catalogue description has to bring some knowledge with him.

If you adopt the policy that the condition of the object will be described as either *pristine, excellent, good, fair,* or *poor* (corresponding to school marks of *A, B, C, D,* or *E*), you can save some space. A good practice is to assume that all objects in the collection are in good (*C*) condition unless otherwise indicated, and again you save space.

Measure accurately. On large objects, measure to the sixteenth of an inch, and on very small ones, measure to the thirty-second. You could steal a march on most museums by starting your new registration system with the metric system and measuring to the millimeter. It is best to take the over-all outside measurements in a particular order. If you measure the width first, then the height, and then the depth—and follow that order for everything measured—it will help when making up exhibits.

If the museum receives a number of objects that are more or less alike, it helps to accession them consecutively. Pick the one object that is typical of all of them and describe it in detail. Then, for the rest, use the abbreviation *ibid.*, which stands for *ibidem* and means "the same thing." *Ibid.* refers only to the description immediately preceding it. If you get a dining room set with twelve side chairs, you pick the most typical chair and describe it, and then, for the others, you need only mention minor variations after the word *ibid.*

Even if the objects being accessioned are not enough alike to use the word *ibid.*, it helps to line up similar objects. Then similar or unique characteristics will show up immediately. If you are accessioning a group of costumes, place all the dresses in one pile, all the coats in another, and so on, instead of just grabbing items at random, as they come out of the trunk. You will be amazed at the way this simple arrangement helps descriptions. All of this is especially true of uncatalogued (that is, unaccessioned) collections.

You may have a difficult time telling some museum people this, but one table is pretty much like another, one plane is very much like another, and one dress is very much like another. Do not waste time describing the obvious. Describe the unusual characteristic and the distinctive ones that mark the object. Some objects, such as stamps and coins, are described in catalogues. Referring to the catalogue number can simplify descriptions. Some classes of object have a standard scholarly work written about them. Reference to the description in that work can save time.

Do not make up words for technical descriptions. If you do not know what a ferrule is, call it a band of metal. There are many technical terms that help, but even if you do not use them, using plain explanatory terms instead, your records will be just as accurate as if you had expressed everything technically. Consistency and accuracy are more important than a technical vocabulary.

Almost anything in the world can be described while standing on one foot. The second the other foot touches the ground, stop describing.

Head

Eye
Nose

Ear
Lobe
Jaw

Cheek
Mouth
Tooth

Neck

Shoulder

Lip
Chin

Body

Arm
Wrist
Hand
Knuckle
Finger
Waist

Elbow

Skin

Knee

Leg

Foot
Sole
Toe

Joint
Heel

Although most objects have technical terms attached to them, novices in the registration field will find it easy to describe objects if they use the parts of the human body and certain articles of clothing. Developing a technical vocabulary is important for accurate descriptions. Body parts not normally used are *ankle, trunk, palm, thumb.* Sometimes it is also useful to indicate directions, such as *top, bottom, side, front, back, end.* Commonly used names for parts of garments are *jacket, sleeve, skirt, cuff, pocket, belt, shoe, button.* Such terms as *the whole, part,* can be used to refer to the object in general. You can also use letters of the alphabet—A, B, C, and so on—as identification aids.

Nomenclature

Since almost all the categorization of the collection done after the accessioning is based on what we call the object and the way it is described, a great deal of attention must be spent on naming and describing. When we get to catalogue, we will try to show how a catalogue may be arranged by the word or title given each object. It will only cause confusion if more than one name is applied to an object.

If you know quite a bit about furniture, you might describe a typical large case piece as either a Kass, a Schrank, a Wardrobe, a Press, an Armoire, or whatever. Even if catalogue cards bearing these descriptions are all filed under "Wardrobe," this is bound to cause some confusion. The answer is to use only one description for one type of object.

If you do not know something about a class of objects, the problem gets worse. People who do not know anything about tools tend to class all wooden planes as "block planes." A block plane is only one specific type of plane and became common when all-metal planes were introduced in the 1870s. To confuse matters, there are some wooden block planes. The rest of the planes all have certain definite titles, based on function. In describing clothing, the type of cloth, the cut of the pattern, and the method of assembling the pieces all become important for descriptions, even though, I dare say, most male curators are ignorant of such subtleties, as most women curators may be ignorant of tools.[1]

Until now, the history museum has been somewhat at a disadvantage when compared to art museums and science museums, which have a standardized nomenclature. That is, of course, more true of a museum of science than one of art, but there are some commonly-agreed-on terms for types of art objects that are almost standard. History museums did have some standardized nomenclature available to them, especially in the areas of furniture, tools, and textiles, but most of the objects do not have standardized nomenclature. What is the difference between a skillet and a frying pan? Or a carpet and a rug? A car and an automobile?

1. Before I am jumped on about assigning roles by sex, let me state that the tool collection at Old Economy was very capably catalogued by a woman.

In large museums, each speciality has an expert, and that problem is somewhat taken care of, but in the small museum the curator has to know everything—which is impossible.

A recently published book by Robert G. Chenhall, *Nomenclature for Museum Cataloguing* (Nashville: American Association for State and Local History, 1977) gives the necessary rationale and procedures for setting up a nomenclature for your museum. He also lists tables of words in order to establish a standard museum nomenclature. It would be helpful if administrators of all museums, no matter how small the museum may be, carefully read and followed this book. The system as it is outlined may be too complicated for the needs of the very small museum, but it should be followed as closely as possible. It will furnish a standard terminology when you are talking to other museum people; it will keep the catalogue consistent throughout the administration of several curators; and it will greatly facilitate the computerization of the catalogue.

The easiest way to implement a nomenclature is to refer to Chenhall's book when the accessioning process is begun for any object. If the name of the object is carried in the book, an entry should be made in the museum lexicon when the object is accessioned. For instance, if you find that you are accessioning a card table, you would place an entry in your lexicon on "table, card" under recreational devices and equipment. If you find that you have a strange type of plane called a "jack rabbet," that is not carried in the Chenhall book, you must create a new entry under planes, "Rabbet, jack," in the tools and implements section.

The *nomenclature* is the actual list of words and the *lexicon* is the method for storing and retrieving this list. For all practical purposes, the lexicon of a small museum will be a file drawer.

An easy way to set up a museum lexicon is to have a three-by-five-inch card file. Each time you must create a new word in the lexicon, you print it on a slip of paper and file it. I would use paper rather than a card, as paper takes up less room. If you place the accession number of the "first use" of the word, it will be a help in later descriptions. The first use is technically the first time you use that word in your nomenclature. If your collection has been previously catalogued, your "first use" may be the first time you run across the word, rather than the first time it is actually used.

Even in a large collection, the curator will quickly become familiar with all the terms he uses in the nomenclature. A quick reference to the list will be needed to make sure that it is kept up to date and is accurate and complete. Such a nomenclature actually takes little time to implement if you develop one from the very beginning of the museum's registration system. If you already have a large catalogue, developing a nomenclature may be a real problem requiring a complicated system of cross-referencing. Cross references would be required if you used more than one term to describe similar objects—not a good practice, if it can be avoided. It is to alleviate the problem of multiple names for museum objects that Chenhall has developed his system.

If you do have a large catalogue, it may be better to set up the nomenclature for all new accessions and go back and bring your old accessions terminology into the new system when you have time.

The Collections Register

Any system you are going to use will require a collections register. The easiest form to use is a record book that you can buy in any stationery store. You should buy the type that is used to record the minutes of large corporations. It should be of a low-acid, high-rag-content paper, such as Permalife, and it should be well bound. It will cost quite a bit more than the cheapest on the market, but it will last longer. This register will be a permanent record, and the time to economize is not when you are buying it.[2]

Another alternative is to type the collections register and bind the pages. Again, this approach, too, should be carried out on high-rag-content paper. The register should be bound eventually and not placed in a loose-leaf notebook. I am mentioning this

2. These books are listed in office supply catalogues as "minute books." The pages can be removed for typing, if you wish, but they can be permanently sealed in, which is what you need.

as an alternative, as loose sheets tend to be misplaced, which is a bad thing for your primary records.

There are several different methods of writing a collections register, but all notations in it should be in indelible ink. India ink is good; felt-tip pens are bad, as they tend to bleed through the paper. The small museum might find a bookkeeper's ball-point pen adequate, particularly if a backing sheet is placed beneath the page being written on, so that an impression will not appear on the page below. I use an inexpensive fountain pen with an ink cartridge. These can be bought for about a dollar. Use permanent black ink, so that, if the book gets wet, it can be salvaged. The good paper and the permanent ink can be read even if the book is badly soaked and burned in a fire.

I am going to suggest three different accessioning systems, from simple to complex. You do not have to use the simple numbering system with the simple accession system. The Three-Number System may fit the One-Book accessioning method, and

Keeping the registers is an important part of the registration process. In this illustration, entries to the register are being made by hand with India ink. The register in question is a loan register.

Accession files do not have to be elaborate. All the correspondence and documents on each accession can be filed by year. The file in the photograph holds all the accession and loan documents accumulated over fifty years for a collection of more than 25,000 objects.

the One-Number System may fit the more complex accessioning method. The collections register contains the primary information for your registration system. It insures that only one number is issued for each accession, that there are no gaps in the record, and that all the basic information is in one place. I cannot emphasize enough the importance of the collections register. Do not fail to keep it up. It will promote accuracy, consistency, and completeness.

The One-Book Accession System

The easiest system to use is the one in which you place all of your information in the collections register. You would then not have any of the paraphernalia of registration, such as an accession book, cards, and catalogue.

This is rather a radical departure from tradition, but I wonder if the small museum needs so many records. In a collection of less than two thousand or three thousand items, the people in charge of the museum surely will "know" every item in the collection. Why have a catalogue, under these circumstances? You must have good records, but you can have them without catalogue cards and all the other materials. It would be better to have one *good* record and spend the time normally used in typing and shuffling cards doing things more meaningful to the museum, such as getting more artifacts. The system shown here can be improved at any time, as all the basic information will be there.[3]

You need to have these things on any accession record: accession number, title, description, source, provenance, date of acquisition, other information. This can be in almost any order, so long as it is consistent for all objects in the collection.

A typical page in a collections record would look like this:

77.1 Basket:
Split oak; painted green;   *Gift:* Mr. and Mrs. Adam
inverted bell shape; two handles   Smith, 123 Nation Drive,
on rim; bond on edges; some splits Acme City, Pa. 15000
but otherwise in good condition;   9/6/76
approximately 17 1/2" x 16"
diameter.

77.2 Redware Bowl:
Turned-over lip;   *Gift:* Same
tapers from top to base; bottom
flat; inside brown slip, outside not
glazed; inside bottom somewhat
crazed but otherwise in good condition; 16 1/2" diameter x 7 7/8"
high; greatly resembles *75.20.*
Typical local redware of early 19th
century.

3. It is true that if the collection grows, one will need a catalogue and probably cards. If the museum has not made them out, you face the task of going back through your records and making cards on all existing accessions. I still think it best that a museum with a small collection spend more time developing its collection, exhibits, and program, and leave the catalogue until later. When I speak of the curator's "knowing" his collection, I do not mean he does not need a registration system. The museum may not need a catalogue just yet, but does need accession records. The carrying of the records of the museum in the curator's head is what is wrong with many catalogues.

77.3 Candlestick:
> Brass; urn-shaped
> stem; flaring top; stepped circular
> base; 7 1/4" high x 4 3/4" diameter
> at base; base somewhat bent.
> Belonged to donor's grandmother,
> Mrs. John Adams (nee Rebecca
> Smith, 1856-1926).

Gift: John Q. Adams,
15335 Braintree Road
Hero, Pa. 15555
2/10/77

77.4 Curtain Tieback:
> Brass with iron
> back; brass shaft and iron screw
> point; design on a disc and is urn
> in concentric rings, one of which
> has a design of a series of cast
> balls; 2 1/6" diameter x 3"; pur-
> chased as one of a set of three
> from Raw Greed Antiques, $6.00
> for the set; money was donated;
> purchased to match existing house
> tiebacks.

Gift: Mrs. Gravely Driver,
3 Lawn Drive,
Acme, Pa. 15000
4/13/77

77.5 Ibid.
> (*Ibid.* stands for *ibidem* and means
> "the same thing.")

77.6 Ibid.
> 2 1/4" diameter

77.7 Syrup Jug:
> Silver; rounded middle,
> tapering at bottom and flaring at
> top; base 2 15/16" diameter;
> curved handle and lip; hinged
> fitted lid; lid has small spherical
> stem. $28.00

Purchase: Wattagyp
Antiques, 9234 Struggle
Way, Hero, Pa. 15555
8/19/77

All the information you need is readily available on this form. There will be other information in the accession correspondence file. The information is lined up in the order in which you will usually need to know it—the accession number, the object, the description, the method of acquisition, from whom and where it was acquired, and the date. Methods of handling the One-Number and Three-Number systems are shown in other places, but are essentially the same. The reason for lining the information up in columns is that sometimes you are going to be interested only in the number, sometimes only in the object, sometimes only in the source. The description is often the last thing you will be looking for, but it is readily available.

Putting all of your information in one book has some advantages to the small museum. The main advantage is that it prevents your having to handle a lot of paper. The second is that it is self-explanatory. Anyone following can easily figure out what you were doing. The third advantage is that all the information you need for the most complex registration system in the museum field is all there. If you ever wish to develop a catalogue, you can type cards quite easily from such a record. This is especially true of making a donor catalogue, which is one of the most important catalogues in the museum.

The disadvantage is that it is only one record. It is convenient to be able to compare one record with another to find discrepancies. All systems develop discrepancies, and you have to get them out. Finding them is easier when you have more than one record. On the other hand, the more records you have, the more likely you are to have discrepancies, and the one-record system is as close to a self-correcting system as you are going to get.

We have spoken of it as a One-Book System, but you should have more than one copy. At the end of each year, you should have your records microfilmed or have a Xerox copy of them made, and the copy should be stored in a safe place. This safe place is a separate building, preferably not in the museum complex (if you have a complex), and it should be fireproof, so that your records will survive any disaster.

The records of the museum are only tools meant to help you preserve and interpret the collection. Do not create a monster that will eat up the purpose of the organization in a maze of paperwork. Simplicity is the word.

The Two-Book Accession Record

There are several reasons for having your registration system in several drawers, so to speak. The main reason is that it makes possible the checking of one record against another. A second reason is that you can divide your records into two or more functions so you are not handling your whole registration system every time you have to look something up.

This first basic division of records beyond the One-Book System should be to segregate the register from the accession records. The Collections Register then becomes a ledger to keep track of accessions, accession number, and donors, and the accession record contains the detailed information about each accession. The Collections Register would contain almost all the information it held before, except for the description of the object and the address of the donor. The Collections Register would look like this:

No.	Item	Source	Date
77.1	Basket	Mr. and Mrs. Adam Smith, gift	9/6/76
77.2	Redware Bowl	Same	9/6/76
77.3	Candlestick	John Q. Adams	2/9/77

The advantage of having such a Collections Register is that each accession can be entered in it as the item is acquired, and the accession records can be made up later. One person can make up the Collection Register, and another can make up the accession. If the accession record is lost, the register can be made up again, and *vice versa*.

The accession record under this system would look exactly like the one in the One-Book System. A separate sheet should be made up for each accession. An example of a typewritten accession sheet, using the Three-Number System, appears on the following page.

EXAMPLE OF TYPEWRITTEN ACCESSION SHEET
(Using Three-Number System)

February 11, 1975

Gift of: Mr. and Mrs. Loyal Descendant
(in name of Mrs. Noble Ancestor)
123 Beesom Street
Hero, Pa. 15555

75.11.1 BROOM-MAKING MACHINE: Meant to fit on bench; consists of a rotating clamp held by a rachet; clamp is hollow to hold broom handles; in back is device to hold wire, consisting of a crank-turned square on which slides a wooden spool; cast iron on wood base; base vaguely L-shaped; whole painted black; 37 1/2" x 27 1/4" x 10 1/2" over-all.

75.11.2 BROOM-MAKER'S VISE OR CLAMP: Meant to clamp flat brooms for sewing; consists of two iron jaws worked by lever; jaws can be raised and lowered by ratchet and crank mechanism on left side; one guide (right rear) broken; whole stands on two pieces of wood to working height; moulded into lips of jaws is "Pat'd Sep. 10, 1876"; painted black; 43 3/4" high x 14" x 30" deep (less handle) over-all; 34" to top of handle with jaws closed.

75.11.3 BROOM CUTTER: Consists of a tapered wooden trough; at small end is a cutter, cast iron, that pivots at one end and is worked by a handle; a series of holes is drilled in cutter, which reads "W & D York Pa"; meant to sit on legs; painted black; 44 1/4" x 28 1/2" x 12 1/2" over-all with handle down.

NOTE: The above items belonged to Mrs. Descendant's great-uncle, William Jones (early twentieth century), a broom-maker who built house at 123 Beesom Street in 1920.

acc/DBR/mc

All the information you need is in this book. There are several ways to keep the accession book. The simplest is to write it out in ink and by hand. A better system, I believe, is to write or type these records on single sheets of 8 1/2-by-11-inch paper of high quality following a form similar to that in the example. At the end of some period of time, usually a year, these pages should be bound. Again, the paper must be a good, low-acid bond paper. Until records are actually bound, you must be careful not to lose a sheet, since that could really mix up your records. You can, of course, go back to the Master Record and re-create the accession record, but even if the possibility of that occurs, you are doing something incorrectly.

There are a few advantages of having your accession records on separate sheets. One is that, until it is bound, you can make duplicates easily (also on bond paper). The second is that it is neater—neatness is part of accuracy. Another is that you will find it is easier to shuffle single pages of your records.

One problem with these One- and Two-Book systems is that you have all of your information in a book. If you need information on a single item, you must go back to the whole book (or more). If that happens frequently, you should start thinking of more complex systems.

The Multirecord System

If your needs pass the simplicities of records that can be contained in bound books, you need to think of using cards. Many people, some of them professionals of high standing, think that a registration system cannot exist without cards. I have tried to show that that is possible. There is nothing wrong with cards, per se, so long as you do not let them use so much of your time that they eat up your records.

We are going to discuss catalogues in the next chapter, but here the only extra record we will discuss is the Accession Card. The Accession Card contains exactly the information that is in the Accession Record, whether it is the One-Book or the Two-Book System. The card should be filed by category or location of the object, as your needs dictate. The major reason for having a card is that you have to handle only the one card with

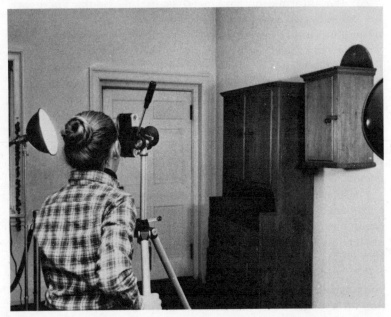

Photographs of the collection do not have to be of any artistic merit. They should be good photographs and show all the features necessary for a description, but they do not have to win a prize for artistic quality.

the object, not your whole record-keeping apparatus. It can save wear and tear on the records. It is also possible to make notes on the card without disturbing your original records. If the card is lost, it is easily replaced.

There are other records that can be considered part of the accessioning process. One very important one is a photographic record.[4] It is a good practice to photograph important items in your collection, and photographing the entire collection is a good idea. Photograph only one object at a time and photograph important details separately. Black-and-white film is best. The photographs should be filed by accession number and are an important part of your records. The negative should be carefully saved, as well as a positive. (See chapter 5.)

4. Jansen L. Cox, "Photographing Historical Collections: Equipment, Methods and Bibliography," *AASLH Technical Leaflet #63* (1973).

Putting the number on the object is one of the most important parts of the registration process.

If something is stolen, you can furnish the insurance company with a photograph and a description. A picture is worth a thousand words, and photographs help greatly in visualizing the object.

The value of an object is sometimes part of the description. With two seemingly identical objects, one might be valuable and the other without value. As an example, two identical smoothing planes might vary in price by a hundred dollars. One of them might be an Auburn, of which there are numerous examples, while the other might be one of three lesser-known examples of an otherwise unknown maker.

In this instance, the current market value, or an indication of it, might be an important part of the description. The problems with evaluating an object are that the person doing it has to know the market well, the values are always changing, and an object might be valuable to you and not valuable to someone else.

If a money value is part of the description, it is best to indicate that in pencil on the accession record. That way, if the value changes, it can be changed on the records. Some museums list the monetary value for every object in their collections, and some do it for only some of the items held.

Placing the Number on the Object

An important part of the accessioning process is the placing of the accession number on the object. Everything done, up to that point, has been done on paper, *but all the work will be wasted if the object is not numbered.* The number associates the object permanently with its records. It should be easy to find, yet inconspicuous. It should be permanently attached, yet not utterly impossible to remove.

It is important to be consistent in placing the numbers. Always try to put them in the same location on the same type of object. The museum field is developing a standard of always placing the number on the lower right side whenever possible; but I object to the placing of numbers on finishes of furniture or the working surface of tools, and therefore believe that hiding the number is best so long as it is not hidden too well.

There are many methods available, and Dudley and Wilkinson[5] illustrate a number of them. There are several easy methods that are quite satisfactory and readily available to even the smallest museum. The best method is to use paint. A high-quality sign-painter's enamel kept in a small container and applied with a very small brush (#000 or #0000) makes a very satisfactory number. A little practice is necessary to get it right. Red is the most commonly favored color, with white second. The numbers should be visible without being conspicuous. Covering the painted-on number with clear nail polish or clear lacquer will help to preserve it. Nail polish is a very high-quality lacquer or synthetic.

Another method that is satisfactory, especially for glassware

5. Dorothy D. Dudley and Irma B. Wilkinson, *et al., Museum Registration Methods,* revised edition (Washington, D.C: American Association of Museums, 1968).

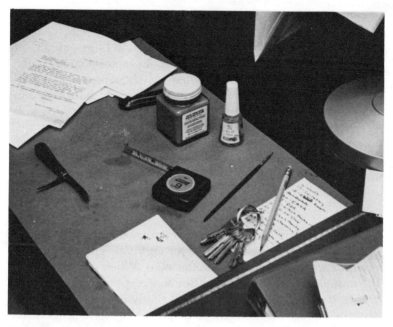

This is a candid shot of the equipment actually used to accession an object and mark the number on it. Paper, pens, a rule, a brush, paint, and nail polish are all that is required. The object being accessioned is the pocket knife illustrated elsewhere.

and china, is to paint a small stripe of high-quality clear nail polish on the object, write the number on it in India ink, and then apply another stripe of clear nail polish to cover and preserve the number.

For clothing and fabrics, the best method is to sew on a small strip of cloth tape with a basting stitch and write the number on it with a laundry pen. On clothing, it is a good idea to sew the tab in the neck or in the waistband. On large pieces of fabric, such as rugs or coverlets, it is a good idea to sew tabs on opposite corners so they can be found easily.

The number should be put in an inconspicuous place. On furniture, it can be placed on the back and inside drawers. The number can go on the bottom of china and glassware. On things such as tools and small objects, try to decide how you might display them and place the number where it will not be seen. It is a good practice to place the number in several places on large objects.

A very large object, such as a vehicle or farm equipment, might have a brass tag screwed on in an inconspicuous place. Sometimes it is a good idea to place a lowly paper tag on an object in storage so you can find the number easily, but never consider such tagging a substitute for placing the number on the object permanently. Labeling machines that print letters and numbers on long strips of plastic turn out very readable labels but are unsatisfactory for permanent labeling, and the adhesives might be harmful to the surface of the object.

De-Accessioning

There is hardly a museum in the country that does not depend on the good will of its audience for survival. That good will is often expressed in gifts to the museum. When offered objects, the museum is under an obligation to accept only what it really wants, can really take care of, and really intends to keep. It is poor policy for the museum to dispose of articles in its collection unless there is an overriding reason for doing so. That is especially true if the item was a gift. Strong enforcement of the museum's collection policy should keep the practice of deaccessioning to a minimum.

When you take something into your collection, you should at the same time think about how it might be removed without creating confusion in the records. For one reason or another, objects get broken or stolen, or they wear out. Occasionally, something that does not fit your collection creeps in, like a duck among the swans. If that happens, there should be a clearly understood policy about how the object is to be disposed of. The governing body should make that policy a part of the registrar's manual. Any action to get rid of an object should be done only after the governing body acts.

The easiest way to get such action is to have the curator or collections committee make a recomendation to the board that the object be disposed of and give instructions on the method of disposal. If the board approves, the action is carried out.

You should not get rid of the records for an object that has been disposed of just because the object is gone. You are still obligated to keep the record of it. A note indicating that the object has been removed should be made in red ink in the master record and in the accession book. The type of removal (stolen, broken, sold), the date it happened, and the date of the action of the governing body should all be entered in the permanent record. If you have a catalogue, the cards for the disposed-of object should be removed and discarded. If you want to keep a "dead" file for such catalogue cards, they can be placed in that. The reason for using red ink for this transaction on the records is that it will show up clearly. India ink should be used.

It is poor policy for a museum that depends on gifts to sell items from its collection. Potential donors will wonder if the things they give might be sold. If they give money to buy items for your collection, they might wonder what will happen to their gifts. It is best to sell nothing. However, if you must sell, try to make sure that the donor knows, *before* you accept the object, that you have the option to sell. Use the money from the sale to buy something that will carry the original donor's name.

The worst possible reason for getting rid of anything is a change in taste. If the museum once acquired a group of objects now considered to be in poor taste, it still should keep them. The wheel of fashion turns slowly but surely, again and again, to the same spot. If you dispose of items from the collection solely on the basis of taste, *you* might be considered the philistine—not the person who acquired them! That is why museum management must be very careful about what is accepted for the collection and what is rejected.

Although the museum board should reserve the right to dispose of the collection in any way it sees fit, in actual practice the museum will be rated on how much it keeps and keeps well; and it will be criticized when it gets rid of anything for any reason.

The Final Word on Accessioning

Several different systems of accessioning have been outlined here, in the hope that an understanding of all of them will help the person in charge to set up his own system. The important things about any system are:

1. *That the flow of actions be orderly and uncomplicated from the first contact until the object is displayed or stored.*
2. *That the museum be able to account for any action at any stage of the process.*
3. *That any system used be consistent.*
4. *That the system have the understanding and approval of the people managing and running the museum and the capability of being carried out over a number of years.*

5

Cataloguing

■ If you want to know something about chairs, bring all your chairs together in one place. You can then see the size of your collection, its condition, its strengths and weaknesses, and any other factors for which you are looking. In actual practice, it is easier to handle cards. Despite all the disparaging things I say and think about catalogue cards, the lowly card is often the best

Until the world is made new again, catalogue cards and drawers are part of the registration process.

way to divide a collection into useful increments. It is often the only way.

What is a catalogue? *Catalogue* obviously is related to *category*. They are derived from Greek roots meaning "to enumerate," and "an assembly." *Cataloguing* simply means dividing the records into separate meaningful subdivisions. As a matter of fact, your accession book can be considered a catalogue with everything arranged sequentially by accession number. If you want to know what is associated with a certain number, you can easily look it up in the accession book. Do not confuse the catalogue with the accession records.

The catalogue is made for easy use. It is meant to provide information, and it is used frequently. A catalogue will eventually wear out. Almost all the other records in the museum registration system are meant to be kept forever, but not the catalogue.

What does a catalogue tell you? That depends on what you want to know. It can tell you many things. Before you start to develop a catalogue, ask yourself, "What does the museum need to know?" The most logical thing to want to know is the title of or the subjects in a collection. You may also want to know who used a specific object there or who made it, where it is from, what style it is, what color, where it is displayed or stored, who gave it to you, where the photograph of it is, what material it is made of, or other bits of information. A museum may have one catalogue or twenty catalogues—the number depends on what you need to know and the staff you have to maintain the catalogue.

Main Entry

Librarians have ideal catalogues. They have author, subject, and title catalogues neatly cross-referenced. They have a mysterious thing called a "shelf list." All the items in a library collection are about the same size and are easily stored. The libraries' catalogue techniques are excellent and can be adapted to a museum. The library catalogue is keyed to two things: the catalogue number and the main entry. The main entry in a library is usually the author card. Museums will often find that the title of an object makes a better main entry. The reason for having a main-entry card is that you have one card as a standard. If you need more than one, you just copy the main-entry card and adapt it for each catalogue. Incidentally, your local librarian may be the best person to talk to before setting up a catalogue. The librarian should know the latest techniques and short cuts. The library's catalogue number is partly descriptive, but that does not work too well with museums.

In the museum's case, the main-entry card may be the only card needed, but it would be filed under the name or title of the object, such as *Shotgun*. The filing system is simple and would start with a major category, followed by the secondary category, the tertiary category, and so on. Using tools as an example, you would have headings that look like this:

TOOLS

Blacksmith
  anvils
  bellows
  hammers
  tongs

Carpenter
  chests
  hammers
  measuring
    squares
    rulers
    tapes
  planes
    bench
    molding
    rabbet
    etc.
  saws

It is easier if you color-code your dividing cards so that you can tell the main headings from the subheadings. Cards are filed by accession number within each category.

Many museums have a separate listing of their catalogue headings. These listings are often made part of the registrar's manual or operating procedures of the museum. That helps to avoid duplication, is especially handy with a large staff, and is necessary if the museum is developing a nomenclature for computerization. However, I really do not think a small museum has to worry about listing its headings separately. That is just one more thing to take care of, and if you really want to know what your headings are, you can look in the catalogue drawer.

You will notice that *hammers* appear in both the carpenter and the blacksmith categories of the catalogue. You may want to know all about your hammers, and so create a separate hammer catalogue. The tool catalogue itself may be part of a larger catalogue of implements. There are certain other catalogues that you might consider if you need them and can keep them up.

Once the catalogue has been created, it can be used in preference to the permanent records.

Libraries are different from museum collections and need different registration processes, even though they are an important part of a museum collection.

Location Catalogue

One of the things you may need to know is the location of each object in your collection. It is possible to write the location in pencil on the main-entry card. Another method is to have a card filed by location. When you move the object, you move the card. This is handy when someone asks you about the spittoon in the main room. You can find the card on it easily. These cards help when you begin to write catalogues of exhibits and when objects are stolen. Good museum practice requires that you can place your hands on any object on short notice.

Typing and copying catalogue cards is a real chore, and anything that will make the job easier is to be recommended. It is better to make a carbon copy of one card than to type the same information twice. Museum administrators should consider automatic typewriters and card copiers.

Donor Catalogue

Another primary record that most museums find useful is a donor file. Actually, what you want is a source file, for if you purchase objects, you will want a handy reference to that source, as well. Museums that depend on donors for most of their accessions will find themselves constantly using such a file. It is easy to make up, as the only information you need is the name of the donor or the source and the accession number. All other information is in the accession records. A donor card would look like this:

> Mr. and Mrs. Mack Truck
> *56.3*
> *62.33*
> *65.99*
> *75.8*

The example shown is from a Three-Number System. On the Single-Number and Two-Number systems, you would have to enter all the numbers in sequence, as in the example:

> Mr. and Mrs. Mack Truck
> *56.3-9*
> *62.33-46*
> *65.9-106*
> *75.8*

The cards can be made up at the end of a year quite easily. There should be only one card on each source. Beyond this, you get into the realm of cataloguing.

Association Catalogue

Part of the information that gives an object value is its association with people, places, or events. That association is often more important than the object. A silk hat is a silk hat, but if it had been *Abraham Lincoln's* silk hat . . . ! An object may have a manufacturer's name on it, it may be associated with a particular event, such as the Civil War, or with a particular place, such as Main Street. Association cards are somewhat like donors' cards, as all they have to have is the accession number. A typical example would look like this:

> Gomorrah Pool Hall
> Main Street, Hero (1929-1976)
>
> 62.29
> 70.2
> 77.38
> 76.99
>
> See Association file of GD Lot (owner),
> Main Street
> Pool Halls, Recreation

When you plan to make an exhibit on Main Street, or on recreation in Hero, or on pool halls, or on G. D. Lot, you can look up the information in your association file. This file is easier to make up if you note on the accession record that there *is* an association file. Someone can then comb the accession records once a year and bring the file up to date.

Other Catalogues

This is a book for small museums, and we hesitate to suggest many catalogues for fear that all museums might think it necessary to adopt all of them, when perhaps it is not. The catalogue is useful only if it tells you the things you need to know, and if a small museum needs a catalogue showing that the furniture it holds is divided by style, it should have that kind of catalogue. If the museum has a large collection of glassware, a glass catalogue might be necessary. As examples of specialized catalogues at Old Economy, we maintain a title catalogue divided by subject, a donor catalogue, a location catalogue on two buildings out of seventeen, a catalogue of furniture with "old" accession numbers, developed about forty years ago, and a tool catalogue. These catalogues were established and maintained until recently without any professional staff but the curator. We feel we need these catalogues and can maintain them. If the staff of the museum feels it needs and can maintain a catalogue it does not have, there is no reason why they could not develop such a catalogue.

Cataloguing Existing Collections

Cataloguing is one method of correcting discrepancies in existing collections. If the existing records are not in too bad a shape, it is better to begin at zero and make a complete and accurate catalogue, rather than to go back and try to correct all of the old accession records. The accession records are your original records, and you do not want to alter them too much, if at all. By making the catalogue complete and up to date, you can keep the accession records as they are. If there are many changes, you can copy the catalogue into an accession book after it is completed, and you would then have both an accurate record and the original records.

I favor this method and have used it in the two collections with which I have had a chance to work

Cataloguing as a Term

It may seem that we are using the term *cataloguing* rather loosely to mean both accessioning and cataloguing. *Accessioning* applies only to the actual process of bringing the object into the collection. Corrections to old collections and bringing new ones up to date are not made on the accession records, but are done in the catalogue. Thus, when you audit an old collection, you often refer to that process as *recataloguing* or *cataloguing*. If the corrections are extensive enough, the corrected catalogue would become your primary record. When a collection is considered to have a complete and accurate registration system, it is often referred to as having a "good catalogue."

Size of the Catalogue Card

A large catalogue card is easier to use than a small one. I recommend a 4-by-6-inch card over the normal 3-by-5-inch one. The main reason is that a great deal more information can be put on the larger cards. The problem with them is that they take larger and more expensive cabinets.

Museums with small collections can think in terms of keeping their catalogues in fiber transfer cases until they can afford steel or wooden cabinets. These transfer cases are readily available at any stationery house and are inexpensive. All-wood (versus part-plastic or metal) cabinets are the best.

Catalogues without Cards

There are catalogues without cards. we will discuss computers below, but that is one kind. Some museums have very static collections or static exhibits. In such instances, it is often better to list the information about the collection on sheets of paper. That would actually be something like an inventory. The arrangement is much less clumsy than a pack of cards. These "page" catalogues can be kept in regular file cabinets and can easily be copied on any office copier. They can be kept in each gallery or room. Their big disadvantage is that a change to any item on the page affects the whole catalogue.

Some museums copy their accession sheets and use them instead of cards. That method has the advantage, again, that the accession sheets can be easily filed in a standard file drawer. This is useful for small collections and for museums with static collections.

If you cannot afford anything better, fiber transfer cases make good file drawers. They are cheap and easily transported. This drawer contains a location catalogue for one building. If you buy permanent file drawers, all-wood ones are much better than metal or plastic.

We have discussed catalogues chiefly in terms of cards. The advantage of cards over inventories is that cards can be shuffled and a change on one card does not affect the whole list.

Some museums do not need a great deal of information from their catalogue. Museums that collect highly specialized items, such as coins or paperweights, may need to list only a few things. A museum of coins might want to know only the country of origin, the denomination, the material, the condition, the size, and the date. All that can be placed on a strip of paper. There are quite a few inventory devices on the market that are made for manufacturers and parts suppliers. These will do quite well for that type of operation. Many library-equipment manufacturers make devices of various kinds to hold strips or small cards, such as those for listing periodicals, that can contain very little information but might hold enough for specialized purposes.[1] Card files of the Rolodex type can hold up to two thousand cards in a file a little larger than your two fists.

The museum has to analyze its needs and decide whether it really needs a card file or if some other system might do as well.

Photographing the Collection

It is a good idea to photograph your collection. That helps in identification and description and is a good record of condition. Large formats are best, but the small museum may find that photographs taken with the ubiquitous 35mm camera are quite adequate for its purposes, and these cameras are much cheaper and easier to use than larger ones. It is best to photograph every item. However, circumstances may dictate that you photograph only the more valuable items.

Set up a certain time to photograph—doing it once a month or once a year might be better than trying to photograph everything as it comes in. A film with a small grain should be used, such as Kodak Panatomic X or even Plus-X. Each item should be photographed individually and details should be photographed separately. A contact print can be made on 8-by-10-inch paper of all the photographs from a roll. If the

1. In office supply catalogues, these items are often referred to as tube reference systems or listing reference systems.

Photographing the collection may appear to call for a lot of complicated equipment. In actual practice, very little equipment or time is needed to photograph at least the important objects in the collection.

negatives are attached to the back of this contact and placed in an envelope, the whole can be filed in a standard file drawer. The drawer should be in a fireproof cabinet, if possible. The accession number can be written near each individual print.

A second contact print can be made and cut up and the individual prints fastened to the front of the catalogue cards for ready identification. A third contact print might be made and filed with the duplicate records of the museum.

This photographic recording is not too difficult to do and will give you a good record. It is one service that can be performed by volunteers, even in large museums. Film is inexpensive, and many photographers will be glad to take the pictures if you furnish the film.

It is only a step from this procedure to the establishing of a separate catalogue of photographs of the collection. Museums that keep these files often have a special catalogue card for their photographic catalogue. An easy system is to fasten the print to a standard catalogue card and note the negative number. These can be filed in any way that the museum feels best, but the easiest system is to file them in numerical accession order.

When we say *fasten* the photograph to the card, we mean glue it. Just any glue will not do, especially rubber cement or library paste. There are library pastes made for archive use that are acceptable. White casein glues are adequate if applied thinly. They are flexible and do not deteriorate with time. If you can dry-mount the photographs to the cards, it is best, but this is time-consuming and takes special equipment. Staples are unsatisfactory as they take up too much room.

If you can have the photographic prints made the size of your card file drawers, the photographs can be filed without being fastened to a card. The information you need can be printed on the back. If you have a rubber stamp made that indicates the information you need, you can make the job much easier A typical stamp might look like this:

| HERO COUNTY MUSEUM |
| Photographic File |
| |
| Acc. *68.26.1* |
| Neg. *030877*[2] |
| *Object Horsehoe* |

This is really all you need in this type of file. There is an example of a photographic catalogue card in the appendix.

Photographs in the Collection

Most museums have photographs in their collection where the photograph itself is the artifact. In libraries and archives there are well-established methods of filing photographs. If you have a large collection of historic photographs, you should consult some of the literature on this.[3] A small museum may have

2. The negative number in this instance is the date that the negative was taken, March 8, 1977. This is a handy way to keep track of these things.

3. Robert A. Weinstein and Larry Booth, *Collection, Use, and Care of Historical Photographs* (Nashville: American Association for State and Local History, 1977). See also Paul Vanderbilt, "Filing Your Photographs: Some Basic Procedures," American Association for State and Local History, Technical Leaflet #36 (1966).

problems with its photograph collection because these photographs are acquired in the same fashion as the rest of the collection. The museum will want to make a place for them without creating a whole new record-keeping apparatus just for photographs. Whether the historical photograph is a gift or a purchase, it should be accessioned according to normal pro-

This is an example of a contact print of a roll of 35mm film that shows photographs of major items in the collection. These can be cut up and individual frames fastened to catalogue cards and/or the accession numbers written on the sheet. These prints are not very high quality, and it is important to keep the negative so that a good print can be made of any frame if needed.

cedure. There also is the problem of how to classify it. If you have an accession such as

> 79.26.33 Photograph: Stamped with the name "Opaque Lens Studio, Hero, Pa."; sepia; group of Hero County Masons at annual picnic, Marsh Park, 7/4/04; picture size 10" x 14," mounted size 14" x 16"

—what is your main entry? Here, an association file can be helpful. The photograph can be placed in a photographic file under its accession number and in an association file on such things as *Masons, picnic, Marsh Park,* and so on, can be made up. Reference to that particular photograph can readily be made by the accession number.

A simpler but less satisfactory system is to file the photograph under one heading, such as *Masons,* and hope that you can find it when you need something on *Marsh Park.*

Historic negatives, particularly glass ones, need highly specialized storage. If you make a print and a film negative, you can store the negative on the back of the print and place it in an envelope *made of inert paper.* Glass negatives should have a paper negative made of them and be stored in the same fashion. If you cannot afford to do that, glass negatives should be stored in inert envelopes by accession number—as safely as you can manage. Photograph supply houses sell special envelopes for that purpose, and they are inexpensive.

Nitrate negatives were used in this century up into the 1930s, especially for movie film. They are very dangerous to store and are highly inflammable. They have a distinctive smell, which you can learn to recognize. They deteriorate rapidly. The ideal system for storing nitrate negatives is to rephotograph them and destroy the originals. *However,* if the original is historically important, you may wish to store it after the copy negative is made. This is a highly specialized area of preservation, and if you have more than a few of these nitrate negatives, you should bring in a knowledgeable consultant. This is one area where grant money is often available to hire consultants and preserve, catalogue, and store historic photographs.

Computerized Catalogues

There is a lot of literature on the use of computers in

museums. This is not a book on computer cataloguing.[4] However, we must discuss a few aspects of computer cataloguing in regard to registration. First of all, even the smallest museum may have access to a computer. Some local bank or industry might provide such access. Many government-run museums, no matter how small, have access to a publicly owned computer. There are small desk-top computers that are ideal for the registration process of a small museum, and many museums can afford them. When the museum sets up the registration process, it might estimate what the process will cost if done manually against what it would cost if done by machine. You might be surprised at which is more reasonable.

Second, we need to keep in mind that there is a lot of difference between a completely automated record-keeping service and an inventory system. The first may be valuable for a large collection with much movement inside the collection; the other is probably more useful for most museums. From an inventory system, you can extract almost any kind of catalogue you wish, if the information is there in the first place.

It is true, too, that it is possible to have an "automated" system without a computer by having your information on IBM cards and by sorting them mechanically. In many respects, this last system is best for the small museum and is within the cost range for many.[5]

Any of the systems proposed here are adaptable for computers. It is important that you be consistent in the method you choose, the nomenclature you use, and, to a lesser extent, the order in which you list the information.[6] Anyone starting a new registration system or working on an old one must keep in mind that someday someone may want to automate the system, even though that may seem unlikely at that moment.

There are mechanical systems like the Royal-McBee System

4. Robert G. Chenhall, *Museum Cataloguing in the Computer Age* (Nashville: AASLH, 1975) is the best for our purposes.

5. Anita Manning's "Data Retrieval without a Computer," *American Association for State and Local History Technical Leaflet #85* (1975), shows a system well worth considering.

6. Robert G. Chenhall, *Nomenclature for Classifying Man-Made Objects* (Nashville: AASLH, 1977) is a book even the smallest museum can use. Note especially what he says about nomenclature.

that use cards punched along the edge and sorted by a device similar to a knitting needle. Such systems have value, but only a limited use in most museum systems.

What Not To Do and When Not To Do It

A mistake people often make about a catalogue is to confuse it with accession records. It is tempting to type up all the accession records on cards, neatly file them in some fashion, and say you have a catalogue. It is equally easy to take a card from the file and lose or misplace it, and you have then lost one of the primary records of the museum. If you are going to have a catalogue, make it separate from the primary records. The catalogue gets used and eventually will have to be replaced, but the primary records should be kept forever.

I realize that I suggested in the One-Book Method that a museum *could* use its accession book or register as a catalogue. That method is for small museums that do not have much need for access to their records and who have a small staff. If you use that system and find that you are going to the register very often or that the register is getting dirty or damaged, it is time to think of establishing a catalogue. You could make a Xerox copy of the register and use it as your catalogue.

Another mistake is to have a different form for each type of catalogue. They proliferate: there will turn out to be a card for the main entry, another for the room catalogue, another for display, and yet another for the phase of the moon. Unless you have a large printing budget and lots of people to shuffle cards, it is better to keep the types of cards down to a minimum. If you wish to separate one type of catalogue card from another, you can color-code them. The card used for your main entry can serve for almost all other cross-references. The donor card can be typed on a blank card, as can the association card. There are sample cards in the appendix.

Summing up: there is a trick to cataloguing. The trick is to do it right the first time. It is a common mistake in cataloguing to start off on the wrong foot, do half the job, drop it, and come back later and start over again. It is better to decide, at the beginning, what you really want to do, begin it carefully, and complete one entire section before going on to the next.

The purpose of cataloguing is to arrange your collection in

usable categories. It is easier to shuffle cards than objects. Museum authorities should decide what information will be needed from the catalogue and then divide the catalogue into those units. There are other methods of cataloguing for the small museum that may be easier to use than cards. In the back of everyone's mind should be the thought that someday all such records may be in a computer. There are mechanical retrieval systems other than computers. The museum must be careful not to create a catalogue-monster that will eat up all the staff professional's time.

6

Documentation

■ When you acquire an artifact for the museum, you acquire a lot more than the object—you acquire the past history of the object and of the people who used it. Such a legacy is often more valuable and more interesting than the object itself and must be carefully preserved.[1]

Much of the information on the new acquisition may be documentary. The person who donates it might also donate letters or printed material associated with the item. Such documents should be placed in the accession file with the accession number carefully noted on them in soft (#2) pencil. All documents associated with the object must be kept in this fashion. Occasionally some archival material too large or too valuable to place in an accession file may accompany a new object. Such material should be located in the museum archives and cross-referenced to the object. It might be a good idea in such instances to place a copy of the accession sheet with the archives.

1. Carl E. Guthe, "Documenting Collections: Museum Registration and Records," *American Association for State and Local History, Technical Leaflet* #11 (Revised, 1970) is actually a whole registration process that would insure adequate documentation.

Some information about the object may not be in written form. The donor may tell you some of the history: "My grandfather used this to build the Hero Town Hall." When something like that happens, learn what he knows about his grandfather, note it carefully, and place it in the accession record; it will give you clues on where to look for further information, later on. The person who makes the contact should get all the information the donor has. Even if the donor is not sure of details, every fragment should be noted. The following is an example of the method of noting information of this type:

> 68.22.3 Hewing ax; Broad ax; iron with steel insert for blade; stamped COLLINS AXE CO; donor says that this ax was used by his grandfather, James Cam (ca. 1810-1888) to build Hero Town Hall, 1868; grandfather was general contractor for hall and this was first big contract grandfather ever had (see Smigg's History of Hero County, II, 698); and that joists, plates, and rafters were hewed along Turgid Creek; head is 16" x 9 1/4" x 1 1/2"and handle (hickory) is 24" long overall.

I have qualified several statements in this description. I use the statement "donor says . . ." A tradition almost eighty years old is somewhat suspect, but, after all, it is in his family. The donor did not know the exact dates that his grandfather lived so these are what he recollects and are qualified with the notation "ca." for circa (about).

It is a good practice to research things carefully, make sure of all your facts, and cite all your documentation. In this instance, the contract for the town hall should be found, the exact dates of the life of the original owner established, the Collins Axe Company researched to see if they could have made that ax in 1868, and so on. The small museum may not have the time and the resources to do that much research, but if all the information given by the donor is placed in the records, the bones for the research will be there. With that information, the gift is a valuable artifact for the collection; without it, it is just another ax.

Dealers and sellers tend to build up their products when they sell them. If the dealer has an attribution, he should be willing to back it up. The unsupported statement of a dealer that some object was made in the town and used by someone notable is not worth much. If he is charging for the attribution, he should be able to document it. In the instance of a table said to have been made in the town, the dealer should, at the minimum, be able to show some evidence that the table was purchased by someone who lived there at the time it was made.

Attributions tend to be spread like lard on objects. There is a great deal of difference between a genuine art nouveau lamp signed by Tiffany and a similar one that is unsigned. If the dealer claims the unsigned one is a Tiffany, he should be able to prove it with some sort of documentation that can be put in the files. There is a great deal of difference between something that is signed and something that is unsigned.

The same rules apply to provenance. Provenance is the history of the object, its owners, and the places where it has been. If someone claims that an object has used by a certain person, he should have some evidence of that. In the absence of any written documents, the fact that an object has stayed in one family is pretty good—although not final—evidence of provenance. If someone gives or sells you something from a certain family or place, such evidence as a bill of sale from an auction or house sale is good, but not final, evidence of its provenance.

A certain amount of skepticism toward undocumented attribution and provenance is a good tool for the curator. Unsupported statements should be recorded, but accepted only for what they are—unsupported statements.

Research Files

This is not a book on how to do research. It would be impossible to give a bibliography or list of books that is going to help every museum document its collection. The researching of objects is a specialized form of research, but it is no more esoteric or difficult (and no less) than any other form of historical research. We list a number of sources in the bibliography regarding registration of collections, but the researcher is going to have to develop his own sources. I would like to offer some suggestions.

If the museum is specialized in some area, such as agriculture, a larger museum that has an agriculture collection, research staffs, files, and a library might be willing to help. They are not going to do your research for you, but they will at least help you get started. There are specialized libraries that will have collections in your field. They will often be willing to suggest lines of research. A museum can borrow books through interlibrary loans. There are trade associations that maintain research centers and often have libraries and laboratories. I remember with a great deal of affection all the help the Society of Automotive Engineers gave me when I was once in charge of a vehicle collection. There are large collections of trade catalogues and manuals at the Library of Congress and such places as Eleutherian Mills. Anything with a patent date or number is easy to research. There is hardly an interest so small that it does not have at least two rival organized-interest groups, each with a publication. There are books on just about everything. The best place to start is with the subject index of your local library.

The museum must construct its own research file. The first step is to make up a basic bibliography on the particular area of the museum's collection. These publications, no matter how few, should be assembled in a library.[2] Museums should be members of the various scholarly and interest groups that are concerned with the same area of knowledge as the museum. In that way, the museum can learn about publications in its field. Publishing and remainder houses get mailing lists from these organizations and send out catalogues in which one can often find books on his interest for very little money. The museum ought to have a book budget, no matter how small. I have found that people are quite generous about books and frequently donate them. If you need a book and cannot afford it, make your needs known to the people in your community, and I would be surprised if they do not get it for you. Your local library might be willing to acquire books you are interested in.

2. David Kaser, "The Library in the Small Historical Society," American Association for State and Local History, Technical Leaflet #27 (revised, 1972).

The easiest way to construct a research file is to take each piece of information as it is acquired and create a file on it. As new material is discovered, it can be dropped into the folder or into a new file. Almost everything should be placed in the file—such as quotations from documents, citations from publications, pictures, notes made of conversations, newspaper clippings, and items discovered in research. It is surprising how quickly such a file builds up, and it can be very handy when one has to write something.

Research is not good unless it is published. Even the most modest museum with the use of a borrowed mimeograph machine can turn out a series of guides, catalogues, and special publications.These build up a body of knowledge in the museum's area of interest and increase the museum's stature. The publications, the research file, and the special research library are permanent evidence that the museum is doing research.

Memberships

The primary reason I am writing this book is that at one time in my career I had the good fortune to work for a small historical society and acquired sympathy for, if not under-standing of, these organizations, and I have, since then, been able to advise several small museums. The questions most fre-quently asked by administrators of small museums and societies are those that are common knowledge in the museum field, and the answers are readily available. The information usually wanted is in the literature of the large "interest" organizations. When asked why it does not join these organiza-tions, the small society usually says it cannot afford it!

I think you cannot afford *not* to join. One hundred and fifty dollars' worth of memberships can get you advice worth many times that and can actually raise your income. A small society should belong to these groups:

1. The American Association for State and Local
   History (AASLH)
   1400 Eighth Avenue, South
   Nashville, Tennessee 37203

2. The American Association of Museums (AAM)
   1055 Thomas Jefferson Street, N.W.
   Washington, D.C. 20007

3. Your regional and state museum conference.
   The AAM can provide the name and address of
   your conference.

4. Your state museum association, if there is one.

5. Your state historical society.

6. A regional historical society, if there is one.

7. If you are in a historic structure or district, you
   should join the National Trust for Historic
   Preservation, 740-748 Jackson Place, N.W.,
   Washington, D.C. 20006.

8. There are two large national historic organizations. The one more concerned with American
   history is the Organization of American
   Historians, 112 North Bryan Street, Bloom-
   ington, Indiana 47401. The American Historical
   Association, 400 A Street, S.E., Washington, D.C.
   20003, is more interested in history of the world
   at large but is also a valuable organization to
   which to belong if you can afford it.

9. If yours is a Canadian institution, you should be
   a member of the equivalent Canadian organizations.

10. The most recent *AASLH Directory of Historical
    Societies and Agencies* will list many topical
    organizations by interest group. If you have a
    tool collection, there are national and regional
    organizations. If you have a collection of steam
    engines, there are other organizations with

similar holdings. There are organizations for old
clocks, technology, industrial archaeology,
religion(s), beer, genealogy, buttons, lighting
devices, military history, railroads, racial
history, and on and on.

If your collection is strong in some area, there will be an
organization for it. This may sound like a lot of organizations to
belong to, but it is hardly enough. Each of these organizations
brings its members a community of knowledge about one area.
If you are going to build up a research library, you must know
what is already available and begin from there. I have heard,
over and over again, the statement that "We have not been able
to learn anything about . . ."—when there are several books on
the subject.

These organizations bring you knowledge about books in the
field and a judicious purchase now and then will build up the
museum library to the point where it is useful.

You should go to as many of the meetings of these organizations as you can. Even the most modest society can get one
member to the state museum association meeting and to the
regional one, when it is nearby. You will see that many of your
problems are not unique, and you can learn how others solve
them, or at least learn how to live with them.

By becoming part of the museum and historical community,
you will discover that the field maintains standards, that almost
everyone lives up to them, and that you can, too. The standards
apply particularly to the registration of collections.

What Not To Do and When Not To Do It

One of the biggest failures among staffs of small museums is
not collecting information when it is available. Almost all the
basic information is acquired with the object. If such information is not recorded in some form that is useful to people in the
future, the museum is collecting only the physical object and
losing the history. The notes should be neatly filed in some
logical sequence that is readily apparent to anyone. The best
place to file such material is with the accession description and
the accession file. If it is not collected and filed immediately, it
will be lost.

A second error is to expect someone else to do your research for you. It is a common occurrence for a large museum to have someone show up unannounced and say he is from the Forsaken Historical Society and they have a large lighting collection and could the staff of the large museum tell them all about it! In such circumstances, the only thing to do for the people at Forsaken is refer them to a few reference books and the Rushlight Society. If they had had specific questions about specific items, the large museum would have been able to show them some examples and literature. Small societies may find the large museum very helpful, but they cannot expect some curator to impart knowledge in twenty minutes that it took him a lifetime to acquire.

The third most prevalent error made by staffs of small museums is thinking that what is common knowledge in your community is everyone's common knowledge. Just because everyone in your community knows that the old National Bank Building was torn down in 1903, that does not mean that such a fact should not be in your records. Record *everything*. All information should be in the records.

There are many very small societies that, *in their area of knowledge*, are much better researched and more knowledgeable than the largest museum. That is because they set out to learn all they could about their subject and did so. The greatest historian in the world will not know so much about Hero County as the people of the Hero County Historical Society: they just have to make sure that what they know is written down.

It is important, then, that all of the information that comes with an object is preserved along with the object. The museum administration has an obligation to research its collection and make this information available to others by means of exhibits and publications. The information may be much more valuable than the object itself.

7

Loans

■ Unless the exhibits and the collection are very static, a museum will lend and borrow items. The museum will find that its collection is never complete enough to make up every exhibit. It is good museum practice and good public relations to have exhibits of items from the community. Other museums and organizations will want to tap your resources for *their* exhibits. Items are often lent and borrowed for purposes of study or conservation. The sophisticated handling of loans is part of the registration process. There is something of a difference between things that the museum borrows and things it lends, so we are going to discuss these separately.

Loans Out

When the museum lends or lets items go out as loans, it is much simpler than the "loans in" procedure. First of all, with "loans out," the museum owns the object lent and can set up its own conditions. The museum should have a priority of items that it will lend. Some may be lent to any responsible person, and some may be lent only to another museum. Some may not be lent at all. I see no useful reason for making a list, but loan priorities of a museum must depend on the knowledge and experience of the curator. In a volunteer-run museum, it is best that the board approve all loans.

When the museum management is approached about a loan the person in charge should inform the potential borrower of the conditions required for a loan. When the object is picked up, the museum should require that a loan form be signed. Such a form should include these things:

1. Name and signature of the person actually responsible for the loan
2. The name of the organization he represents
3. Address and telephone number of that organization
4. Name of place where the loan will be held if not at that address
5. What is actually being borrowed
6. Exact dates of the loan period, portal to portal
7. Value of the loan
8. Names of those responsible for the insurance
9. Method of transporting the item and names of those responsible for shipment
10. If the item is to be exhibited or conserved, explanation of the way that is to be done
11. Provisions to receive the object back at the conclusion of the loan period
12. Special provisions that may enter in, such as loans to third parties, photography, special handling, etc.

An example of a form for loans out of the museum is in the appendix.

The museum itself can insure the object lent and charge the borrower for the cost. A more common practice is to require the borrower to insure the object and have him produce proof of insurance. Make sure that the borrower's insurance policy is not due to expire while the object is on loan. In the case of objects of small value where the borrower is well known, the museum might waive the demand for insurance. You really do not want the money—you merely want the object back.

The person who signs for the loan should be the person who is *really* responsible for it—not the person who is picking it up. These are sometimes two different people. The person who picks up the object should also sign, but he may not be the responsible person. If the person borrowing the object represents an organization, he should be responsible enough to place his organization under the obligation of caring for all aspects of the loan.

Make sure that both lender and borrower know how the object is to be transferred and know who is responsible for the transference. If the borrower is responsible, make sure he will move the object with sufficient care, equipment, and personnel, *both ways.*

The date of the loan period should include the date the agreement is made, the date the object is picked up, the dates of the exhibit, if the object is lent for that purpose, and the date it is to be returned. There should not be any confusion about loan dates.

The loan form should state exactly what is being borrowed and what its condition is. Here, your accession records are very handy, as you can place the accession number and a short description on the loan form, instead of a detailed description. Any details of condition should be noted before the object is sent out. The condition should be the same when it is brought back.

It is best if the borrower keep the object in his possession and return it to the museum. Sometimes there is a reason to lend it to a third party. An example would be the school district's borrowing some material and sending it out to the schools. Although third-party loans are usually poor policy, that is not always so, and the museum should handle each such instance on its own merits.

Some museums do not like to have their objects photographed while on loan. That applies especially to works of art. Personally, I do not see what is wrong with photographing items on loan so long as the museum knows what the photograph will be used for; but if the museum has such a policy, it should be clearly stated on the loan form.

If the item requires special handling, should not be in harsh light, must be in a controlled humidity, etc., these conditions should be gone over step by step with the borrower before the loan is made. It is a good idea to go through all the provisions of the loan before the loan form is signed.

As in any other contractual relationship between a museum and the public, the loan policies, the loan form, and the types of liability should be gone over carefully with a lawyer before the museum establishes a loan policy and draws up a form.

Loans to the Museum

You are on slightly different ground when you borrow something. When you lend, the object involved is your property, and you can set the conditions. When you borrow, it is not your property, and you take on a liability. You are obligated to return the loan in the same condition in which you receive it. You are responsible for it so long as you have it. If the owner does not show up to reclaim it, you are still responsible for it. If he appears thirty-three years later, as happened to me once, you are still responsible. Therefore, it is a very good idea to borrow only for specific purposes, such as display, and for a specific time, and to return things as soon as possible.

The loan form used for borrowed items is similar to the one used for loans going out of your museum. In fact, you might be able to make do with a single form. However, the conditions of each loan differ. On loan to your museum, you must provide the protection and insurance. Most museums agree to protect the item as if it were their own and to carry fine arts insurance on it. The owner may want to set other conditions and these should be stated on the form.

The loan should have definite time limits. The provision as to who is going to pick it up and return it should be clearly stated. A loan should not continue for a long period of time—a year is about the maximum. Occasionally, museums borrow items for a longer period of time. One should hesitate to request an unusually long time period, but sometimes there is a good reason: a donor may not have clear title; it may be the only way some rare item can be exhibited; or the museum may hope that the donor will eventually give it if it is kept long enough. These "long-term" loans should be for a period of a year, renewable from year to year. That will remind both parties that it is still a loan—and it will remind you to keep your fine arts insurance up. If you have more than a few of these "long-term" loans, you are doing something incorrectly.

Loan Numbers and a Loan Register

Museums that borrow a lot of material often keep a loan register and assign numbers to each loan. This is a good idea if you are mounting four or six large loan exhibits a year or have a large turnover in your borrowed items. The loan register is kept only for the items the museum borrows. The items the museum lends should already have numbers.

The usual practice is to assign to borrowed objects a number that is exactly the opposite of the one the museum uses for accessions. If one uses a normal accession number, such as 77.26, a loan number would be 26.77. The two can easily be distinguished. Some museums use the prefix "L" on loans, such as L77.26. That also is satisfactory. The loan numbers are attached with temporary tags that are removed when the item is returned. A loan register may look like this:

Number	Borrowed From	Item	Date Received	Date Returned	Loan Form
1.77	Mrs. N. Fingers	Quilt	2/7/77	5/28/77	X
2.77	Lotta Collections	Quilt	2/7/77	5/26/77	X
3.77	Mrs. Mack Truck	Quilt	2/9/77		X
4.77	Mrs. Oleo Margerine	Frame	5/15/77	5/19/77	X

The column for the loan form is checked when the loan form is signed. You will notice in the example that one loan is not marked as returned. The loan register should be checked periodically and the status of all loans cleared. At the end of the year, the register and all loans should be up to date and the loans still in the museum's possession should be listed in the report to the board.

I am only suggesting a loan register, as it is an excellent device to keep track of loans, if you have a number of them a year. I would venture to guess that it would not be necessary if you make fewer than twenty-five or thirty borrowings a year. Whether a loan register would be helpful depends on the staff and the time you have available. Keeping all the loan forms for one year in a file is another way of keeping track of them.

Conservation and Identification Loans

Museums often lend or borrow things for conservation or identification. These transactions are handled pretty much as any other loan. When the museum lends out an object to be conserved, the administration should have a pretty good idea what the conservator is going to do to it. It is a good idea to have the conservator look at the object before borrowing it and then state in writing what he proposes to do. The agreement should be loose enough to allow the conservator some room to work if he runs into problems and tight enough to prevent him from doing more to it than the museum staff wishes. The time limits have to be somewhat looser on these loans as the conservator will sometimes encounter problems, and you do not want to hurry him, but there should be a finite time limit. Loans can always be extended.

Museum staff people will sometimes do conservation work for outsiders. When that is done, the transaction becomes a business deal and not a museum function, and the museum should have the protections that any business has, particularly liability insurance, even if the work is for other museums. One of the ways to justify the cost of a conservation laboratory is the ability to use the excess capacity of the lab for outside work. In those instances, the museum should be as strict on its procedure on the items it takes in as it would be if it were borrowing any other item.

People will often bring things to the museum for identification. It is a good practice to have a policy on that. If the museum accepts the item for identification, it is a loan, just as much as any other loan. It should be treated accordingly. Some museums have a separate form for identification and conservation loans, but I do not think they are necessary.

Existing Long-Term Loans

Museums that have been established for a period of time often have a number of "permanent" or long-standing loans in their collections. It is a common occurrence for such loans to go back fifty years or more. They are a real embarrassment to a museum, particularly as the original donor has a habit of appearing after impossibly long times, or his heirs show up and want their objects back. Even if that does not happen, the object is not yours, and there is always the possibility of its being claimed some day.

Laws vary widely, and there may be a way to acquire legal title. According to the advice I have received, that is difficult, at best, and always subject to question if an heir appears. In one case with which I am familiar, the heirs showed up more than ninety years later. Only the fact that there were twenty heirs and they could not agree on who got the objects kept the items in the museum. Even under such circumstances, such objects are not the museum's nor will they ever be, under present laws.

The best method of clearing such loans is to try to track down the original lenders or their heirs and try to get them to donate the objects or to claim them. That can be a time-consuming and unpleasant task, but it is very necessary. A good procedure for it has been set out by Anita Manning, "Converting Loans to Gifts," *AASLH Technical Leaflet #94* (Nashville: AASLH, 1977).

When you try to clear up long-term loans, you often risk losing a valuable object, but it is better to do that than to offer free storage.

If someone leaves an object at the museum, even without the knowledge or permission of the museum, that object is very likely the museum's responsibility until it is returned. For that reason, it is best to have a policy about what may be received at the museum. This is especially important with volunteer-run museums, where there may be a large number of people working at the reception area over the course of a year. It might be best to have a simple statement placed where every volunteer can see it—a statement such as this:

> *If anyone brings in an object with an offer to donate, sell, or lend it to the Hero County Historical Society, the object may not be left without the permission of Mrs. Supreme Optimist, 728-2208, or Mrs. Usually V. Negative, 266-4500. If they are not available, inform the potential donor that the society may be interested in his object but that you may not receive it and that he should get in touch with either one of those listed above.*

If permission is granted, a simple form can be signed so that both parties know their responsibilities.

In instances such as this, the museum might find it useful to have a "deposit" form that allows prospective donors to leave items at the museum pending acceptance. A form for that is in the appendix.

These deposit forms are very handy when any object is left at the museum and there is no responsible party to accept it. It allows the museum to examine the object at leisure. Unwanted items left at the museum can be returned gracefully.

There is a small historical society to which someone once tried to give 25,000 seashells (all different), weighing 2 1/2 tons. Only chance kept the shells from being left. A procedure such as outlined above can prevent embarrassment.

What Not To Do and When Not To Do It

There is no such thing as a permanent loan—it is either a loan or it is not. Lawyers have a fascinating language. I used to play bridge with two of them and asked them to research our legal responsibilities with regard to loans. One came up with the fact that a loan is a "gratuitous bailment." I liked that. Both agreed that a loan never becomes the museum's property, no matter how long it is kept! As I pointed out, there may be a good reason to take on a long-term loan, but never kid yourself that it is yours. It is best to have such loans on a one- or two-year basis, and then neither party will forget the status of the property.

Do not fail to get everything in writing. Loans are usually made to people with whom the museum is acquainted. There is a tendency to be a little bit careless on procedure when the object has no great value and the deal is between friends. If you *have* a loan procedure, it is a good idea to stick to it. If any questions come up, you will have the details in writing.

Many things that should not be done fall into the curatorial area rather than the area of registration, and so are outside the scope of this book. The person making the loan must insure that the object will be taken care of when it is out of the museum and that the loan will not bring discredit to the museum. For that reason, I am always leery of loans for promotional purposes. You never know, if you lend a carriage to an auto dealer for promotion, that you will not see it prominently displayed in all the media, with the caption "Look at this stupid, creaky old carriage that we got from the musty old historical society. Why drive *this* when you can drive a TOTAL?" It is wise to make sure that any prospective borrower who is unknown to you is actually who he says he is and really does represent the organization that he claims to represent. We usually insist that the borrower write a letter to us on the organization's stationery, stating what he wants to borrow and how he intends to display it.

Loans to the museum tend to be carefully made and cared for until the exhibit is over, and then the pressure is off. You may get a little bit careless then. *That loan is your baby until the owner has it in hand and is satisfied with its condition. Do not relax your care for a minute.*

When a museum borrows or lends an object, then, it places its reputation on the line. A carefully-thought-out loan procedure will prevent most problems. Remember, in 999 cases out of 1,000, things go well. It is the one time when there is a problem that causes all the trouble. The loan policy of the museum should be such that it handles the 999 cases well and has all its homework done for the one problem case.

Recap

■ A good registration system is like money in the bank. Money in the bank gives a feeling of security and confidence and is a cushion against disaster. There is nothing like a good registration system to promote confidence in a museum's staff. When the public, a donor, a visiting scholar, or another museum professional raises a question about the collection, and the staff can produce objects and records quickly, the professional status of the staff and of the museum goes up a notch. This increases the confidence of the public in the museum and its staff. People are more likely to give objects and money if they have confidence in the museum. Governing bodies of museums are more likely to trust the professional judgment of the staff if they have confidence that the collection is being properly accounted for.

Having a good registration system is not difficult, but it may be time-consuming. I hope that this book will help cut the amount of time spent on the registration system. To have a good system, the person who assumes responsibility has to examine the needs carefully, including the future needs of the museum, its present collection and records, and the availability of staff and facilities; and then decide the exact method that the registration system will use. Any system picked will be a somewhat arbitrary choice, but you have to begin somewhere. It is more important to be consistent, accurate, and complete than to favor any one system over another.

Once the needs of the museum have been analyzed, it is important to write a procedural manual that I prefer to call a "registrar's manual," even if the museum will never have a registrar. Then the museum staff, volunteer or professional, must carefully take each part of the collection and make sure that each object is registered properly.

As each new object comes into the collection, it must be carefully registered under the procedures set forth in the registrar's manual. A museum is supposed to last forever. Fifty or a hundred years from now, the people following us will look at our records and know what we have done. We will have performed one of our most important functions, which is to preserve the documentation along with the object.

I suppose an anecdote might be out of place in a book such as this, but an experience I once had might illustrate the attitude you must develop in order to have a good museum registration system. In the late 1950s, when I was a bright-eyed young curator in training status, I catalogued the tool collection at the Detroit Historical Museum. This involved three or four thousand previously accessioned tools. When I was finished, I handed the completed catalogue to the registrar, along with a few cards of objects about which there were "discrepancies." These were tools with two accession numbers, no accession number, or the wrong accession number. Margot Pearsall, then Curator of Social History, who had general supervision of the museum's registration system, asked me what on earth these cards were. When I told her, she sent me back to correct every one of the discrepancies. When I had found all but one or two of them and turned the catalogue in again, she sent it back again and told me to do "all of it." I thought that all but two cards out of four thousand was a pretty good job, but she said no. When I had accounted for the last one, she told me the catalogue was completed.

That is what you must do.

Appendices

■ These appendices contain two registrars' manuals and various forms that museums may find necessary. The first manual (Appendix A) is about the simplest that can be adopted. It would suit volunteer-run organizations or those with a single staff member. The second one (Appendix B) contains a more complete manual that would suit a very active volunteer-run organization or one with a professional staff.

There is no way on earth that I, or anyone else, can write a manual that would suit all museum administrators under all circumstances. These manuals are offered for your adaptation to your own circumstances and collection. That is why we have Appendix C, which contains all manner of forms that you may or may not find necessary. There are four different accession forms, several types of catalogue cards, and a few other forms that you may find useful. There is even a sample annual collections report. It is not necessary that you use all of these, but only those that suit your needs. Citations in parentheses (C-9, C-2, and so on) refer to documents in Appendix C.

I did not put in any manual for the Two-Number System, since I feel that the use for such a document would be limited. It is relatively easy to adapt one or the other of the manuals for that system.

These forms are not sacred religious documents; they can all be changed to suit your circumstances.

Appendix A

Example Of A Registrar's Manual, Using the Simplest Possible System

This is an example of a registrar's manual using the simplest system recommended. In the form shown, it is set up for a completely volunteer-run museum. It uses the Single-Number System. There are only four forms; one of them is a blank sheet of paper, and one is a blank card. You can't get much simpler than that!

Everything in this manual except loans requires the approval of the board of directors at the end of the year. That may seem a little late, to some people, but the formal expression of approval is meant only as supervision by the board and not as anything restrictive. The board must be able to trust its collections committee and depend on it to judge what can be done and what should not be done.

This manual was set up for a museum that already has a collection. If you are starting a new museum, you can eliminate the material on the old collection and make the manual even simpler.

It should be equally easy to add sections on association files and catalogues from the other manuals in this book.

Registrar's Manual

The purpose of this manual is to set up a procedure to insure that the _____ will have a good registration system, that every object in the museum collection will be registered properly and have a proper and consistent number on it, and that all information on each object will be preserved and, in general, be in conformance with the highest standards of the museum profession.

COLLECTION POLICY

The statement of purpose in the Constitution of the _____ states:

[The statement of purpose for the historical agency should appear here.]

[The organization may have a charter, a constitution, and bylaws. The portions of these affecting collections should appear here.]

[If there is a collection policy statement separate from the above, that should also appear here. A sample collection policy statement appears below.]

To direct these aims, the Board of Directors has adopted the following collection policy:

The _____ will collect only those items related to the purpose of the Society and which the Society can actually properly store, preserve, and protect. There will be a Collections Committee that will have the responsibility for developing and implementing a registrar's manual for the museum. This manual will be the collection policy of the museum and will contain the proper procedures. At the annual meeting, the Collections Committee will report for the Board's approval on the state of the collection and on all new accessions for the preceding year.

In pursuance of these policies, the Collections Committee submits this manual to the Board of Directors.

Respectfully submitted,
Collections Committee

Adopted by the Board of Directors on _____.

COLLECTIONS COMMITTEE

There will be a Collections Committee composed of at least four members. The chairman of this committee must be a member of the Board, but any member of the Society is eligible to serve on the committee. The committee will have general supervision of the collection. The Collections Committee is a standing committee under the bylaws of the _____.

REGISTRAR

The Collections Committee, with the approval of the Board, will appoint one of its members as Registrar and this person will be responsible for the care of the records of the collection. The Registrar will serve for an indefinite term at the pleasure of the Board.

REGISTRATION FILE

The Registrar will acquire a good four-drawer, legal-size fireproof file cabinet with a lock. The cabinet should withstand at least 1,700 degrees Fahrenheit for one-half hour and should have an Underwriters' Seal. The Registrar will place all existing records in that file. It will become the "Registration File." The file is to be kept locked at all times. The Registrar will have a key, and there will be one in the Society's safe deposit box. On approval of the committee, the Board may assign keys to other members.

At the beginning of each year, the Registrar will start a file folder identified by that year. All accession correspondence, documents, and other information on accessions in that particular year will go in the file. Other files may be made from time to time as necessary.

ACQUISITION

When a donor offers the museum an item or items, the Registrar will have him sign a "Transfer-of-Title Form" (C-1). There shall be three (3) copies of this form: one for the donor, one for the Society secretary, and one (the original) for the Registrar. No object will be taken into the museum unless this form is signed. All donors should be informed that items are accepted subject to the approval of the Board. The form must be filed in the Registration File.

In the instance of a purchase, the bill of sale and all other documents will be placed in the Accession File. Before the Treasurer disposes of any canceled check, those related to collections should be given to the Registrar for the Registration File.

ACCESSION REGISTER

The Registrar will acquire a well-bound record book for the museum's use. This should be about 14 x 9 inches. The first one hundred pages should be left blank to record the existing collection. At the beginning of the next page, the Registrar will write the year this manual is adopted (_____) and columns for the accession number, the description, and the source (C-2).

The Registrar and the Collections Committee will take the items existing in the collection at the time this manual is adopted and try to correlate them with existing records and record them in the Register in fashion similar to that for new accessions. The accessions existing in the collection will be entered in the front of the book; the new accessions will be entered beginning on page 101. The Registrar will be sure to record all information about the accession, including the address of the donor and the date of acquisition. All entries in the Register will be made in India ink. The file is to be kept in the Registration File.

ACCESSION NUMBER

The Registrar will assign the number one (1) to the first object acquired under the new system, number two (2) to the second, number three (3) to the third, and so on.

At the beginning of each calendar year, the Registrar will start a new page for that year, but the numbers will continue in series.

Old items in the collection will be assigned the number 71.1[1] for the first item, 71.2 for the second, 71.3 for the third, etc., and be recorded in the front of the Register.

The Registrar may not assign a number without having used the last one.

No one but the Registrar may draw numbers.

The number shall be placed on the object in some manner acceptable in Dudley and Wilkinson, *Registration Methods.*

The number shall be placed on all documents associated with each accession and these documents are to be filed in the Accession File.

DONOR FILE

At the end of each calendar year, the Registrar shall make up a file of donors and other sources. The file card shall contain the

1. The number 71 is used only as an example here. You will use the year *before* this manual is adopted for your old collection, if you have one.

donor's name and the accession number associated with each name (C-13). Only one card shall be made on a donor, or at least until it is filled.

LOANS

On loans to the museum, the Registrar shall have the lending party sign the loan form (C-7). This loan may be approved by the Collections Committee and submitted for approval to the Board of Directors at the next regular meeting. Loans may not be approved for more than one year. The Registrar shall advise the Board when insurance is necessary. Items may be borrowed only for exhibit purposes, unless the Board rules otherwise.

On loans from the museum, the Registrar shall have the responsible borrower sign the loan form. The borrower shall furnish the museum with proof of insurance or of financial responsibility for the loan. The loan may be made only for exhibit purposes. Loans for photography, advertising, or promotional purposes must be approved in advance by the Board.

PRIORITY OF LOANS

The Collections Committee shall designate certain items in the collection as "Priority Items." These may be lent only with the approval of the Board of Directors when the Board receives assurance that the Priority Items will receive proper treatment. The purpose of this is to protect valuable and unique items. All other loans may be made in advance of Board approval by following the procedure set forth in this manual.

ACKNOWLEDGMENT OF GIFTS

Each gift shall be acknowledged by a letter from the Collections Committee, thanking the donor for the gift on behalf of the Society. A carbon copy of this letter with the accession number(s) on it shall be placed in the Accession File. All gifts displayed in the museum must bear the name(s) of the donor(s) in this fashion: "Gift of Mrs. XYZ." From time to time the Registrar shall supply the Publications Committee with a list of donors for publication in the newsletter.

DEACCESSIONING

From time to time, the Collections Committee may wish to remove items from the collection for the following reasons: the item was stolen, broken, or is surplus. On recommendation of the Collections Committee, the Board, with two-thirds of the total membership in attendance approving, may declare an item deaccessioned. It is the policy of the _____ to sell as little of its collection as possible. No deaccessioned item may be conveyed in any manner to a member of the Board, a member of the Collections Committee, or to any other office of trust or honor in the Society.

REPORT TO THE BOARD OF DIRECTORS

The Collections Committee shall submit a report to the Board of Directors at the Annual Meeting, stating all new accessions for the year, all outstanding loans, the general condition of the collection, a statement of work achieved, and any other matter they deem necessary (D-1).

COPY OF THESE RECORDS

At the end of the calendar year, the Registrar shall have the accession records for the year microfilmed. This shall include all documents, pages in the accession register, and copies of correspondence. The master copy of this microfilm will be kept in the _____. A Xerox copy shall be made of this microfilm and become the working record of the museum.

OTHER FILES

The Collections Committee may alter this manual or adopt other files and records from time to time with the approval of the Board and these new provisions shall be made a part of this manual.

Appendix B
Example Of A More Advanced Registrar's Manual

This is an example of a registrar's manual using a more advanced system of registration than the one in Appendix A. This manual uses the Three-Number System and has an accession register separate from the accession book.

The manual is also set up for a museum having a professional staff, but it could be used in a volunteer-run museum. The curator is responsible for the collection and only advises the board of his actions from time to time. There is still a Collections Committee. This committee is also responsible for the whole museum and may be called the "Museum Committee." The Museum Committee would have to maintain the registration system in a volunteer-run museum.

Although this is implicit in all manuals of this type, this manual is meant only as a guide and to give continuity to the system. The board has to trust its professional staff to carry out procedures in a professional manner. If the curator is not doing so, the board must find out why. If the curator believes the policy wrong or in need of a change, he must go to the board to get it changed. This is why a lot of things are left unsaid in the manual.

Again, other forms and procedures from the appendix may be added to this manual, or it can be changed to suit circumstances.

Registrar's Manual For The_____

The purpose of this manual is to set up policies and procedures whereby the collection of the _____ may have a good registration system; that every object in the museum collection will be registered properly and have a proper and consistent number on it; and that all information on each object will be preserved and in general will conform to the highest standards of the museum profession.

STATEMENT OF PURPOSE

[The statement of purpose for the historical agency should appear here.]

* * * *

[The organization may have a charter, constitution, and bylaws. The portions of these affecting collections should appear here.]

* * * *

[If this manual has been prepared as a report to the board, the names of the committee members and the date of submission should be here. A good form to follow would be to state at this point . . .]

Respecfully submitted,
Collections Committee

I. M. Acquisitive, Chairman
Mrs. William J. Obstructionist
Mrs. George P. Implementer

Date

Adopted by the Board of Directors on _____

The Curator, as the most senior professional staff member, is in charge of the museum and the collection and is responsible for the condition of the collection. He shall report to the Board at the Annual Meeting on the state of the collection, on all new accessions for the past year, on outstanding loans, on all deaccessioned items, and on any other matter regarding the collection. He shall do this in a written report that shall be filed with the minutes of that meeting.

MUSEUM COMMITTEE

There shall be a Museum Committee that shall have general supervision of the museum and the collection and shall work with the Curator on the maintenance and improvement of the museum. The Museum Committee shall have at least three members. The Chairman shall be a member of the Board, but the other members may be members of the Society.

The purpose of the Museum Committee is to act as a liaison between the museum and the Board and to act in an advisory capacity to the Curator.

ACCESSIONS

The Curator will secure a well-bound record book about 9 by 14 inches, made of high-quality inert paper, and this will be the Accessions Register (C-3). For each accession, the Curator will enter the accession number, the name of the object or objects, the method of acquisition, and the date the accession became the property of the Society.

The Accessions Register shall follow this form:

Date	Item	Source	Method	Date
78.1	A tool box, with tools	Walrus & Carpenter Co.	gift	1/8/78
78.2	4 silver saltcellars	Posterity Fund	gift	2/21/78
78.3	Hero Iron Foundry lard press	Mrs. Yale Princeton	purchase	4/18/78
etc.				

This register is to be kept in the Accession File.

CERTIFICATE OF GIFT

The museum may not accept any gift until the donor signs a Gift Agreement Form (C-1) before a witness. The Curator or some responsible person may sign for the Society. There shall be three copies of this certificate: the original shall be placed in the Accession File; the second copy given to the donor; and the third copy filed with the Collections Report at the Annual Meeting. The museum copy shall be kept in the Accession File.

ACKNOWLEDGMENT OF GIFT

The Curator shall write a personal letter to each donor, acknowledging each gift on behalf of the Board of Directors. Each gift shall be listed in the newsletter.

In the case of outstanding or valuable gifts, the Curator shall notify the Board at the next regular meeting, so that it may take appropriate action over and above the acknowledgment of the Curator.

The accession number shall appear on all correspondence relating to any accession, and a carbon copy shall be placed in the Accession File.

All objects displayed in the museum shall have the name of the donor displayed on the label. In the case of period rooms, a listing of the donors shall appear near the entrance of the room.

ACCESSION FILE

The Curator shall secure a good fireproof, legal-sized, four-drawer file cabinet with a lock. This cabinet, which should be able to withstand at least 1700 degrees F. for at least one-half hour, will become the Accession File and will be kept in the museum office. The Curator will have the key, and another key will be issued to the secretary, who will keep it in the Society's safe deposit box.

At the beginning of each year, the Curator will create a file and all correspondence and documents relating to the accessions for that year will be placed in that file. The Curator may create other accession files as he sees fit.

All primary records of the Society relating to collection shall be kept in this file and the file shall be kept locked when the museum is closed. At the end of each calendar year, the Curator will have the accessions file for that year microfilmed and the negative stored in the Society's safe deposit box.

ACCESSION NUMBER

An accession number shall have three units: each year shall be identified by the digit and unit of that year, the year *1978* being *78*. Each accession shall be numbered sequentially, as it is received. The numbers are drawn from the Accession Register. The second unit will identify each accession. For the purpose of this museum, each single acquisition from a single source at one time will be an accession. If a donor gives (or the museum purchases) items at two or more separate times, these will be two or more accessions. The third unit will be the catalogue number. Each object in each accession will receive a catalogue number. If there is only one item in the accession, it will still receive a catalogue number, in this case *1* (one). As an example, the eighth item in the fourth accession in 1978 will be *78.4.8.*

ACCESSION BOOK

All the accessions will be entered in a book, following the form attached to this book (C-6). The Curator shall secure 8 1/2-by-11-inch 20-pound paper of "Permalife," or similar acid-free paper. All accessions shall be typed in duplicate. At the end of the year, these accessions sheets shall be bound. The original copy shall be stored in the collections file and the copy shall be the working copy.

[If the museum cannot follow the above procedure, the next best thing is to enter the accessions in india ink in a register similar to the Collections Register. We are including a clause that will allow for this method of entering accessions. Be sure that you adopt only one method or the other.]

ACCESSION BOOK

(Note that this is a substitute for the clause above)

The Curator shall acquire a well-bound book similar to that of the Collections Register and shall enter on page one the year *1978* and list the accessions as in the example (C-4). At the end of the year, he will leave the balance of the page blank and will begin the next year on the following page. The Accession Book will be microfilmed at the end of each calendar year and the negative filed by the secretary in the Society's safe deposit box.

CATALOGUES

The museum will have only three types of catalogue cards. These are: the Catalogue Card (C-10), a Donor Card (C-12 or C-13) and an Association Card (C-11). The Curator shall have a catalogue card typed on each individual item in each accession and file these by title. The Curator may create other catalogues as he sees fit.

NOMENCLATURE

The Curator shall develop a nomenclature and lexicon for the catalogue following methods proposed in Robert G. Chenhall, *Nomenclature for Museum Cataloguing.* The catalogue cards shall be filed by subject following the major divisions in Chenhall.

The Curator shall maintain a donor or source catalogue, and this shall be brought up to date at the end of each calendar year.

The Curator shall maintain an Association Catalogue, and this shall be kept up to date with each accession.

PHOTOGRAPHING THE COLLECTION

The Curator shall photograph the major items entering the collection. Three contact prints shall be made of each item. One contact print shall be cut into the individual frames and glued to the back of the catalogue card. The second contact print shall have the accession number of each object written next to it on the print, and this shall be filed in the Accession File. The third shall also have the accession numbers written next to each object and be filed with the Annual Report.

> *[If the museum resources permit, it would be best to photograph all items entering the collection. If that is possible, the clause above should be amended to include this statement.*

LOANS

The Curator may make or receive loans at his discretion, provided that no loan is for more than one year without the advance approval of the Board of Directors. Loans made to the museum shall be for exhibit only unless approved by the Museum Committee.

On loans to the museum, the Curator shall secure a loan form (C-8) signed by all responsible parties. He will be cautious about committing the museum to a large financial or other obligation. He will notify the Society's insurance agent about all loans. In the event that the loan cannot be returned or is held for more than a year, the Curator shall notify the Museum Committee.

On loans from the museum, the Curator shall have all responsible parties sign a loan form (C-9). He shall ascertain whether the borrower is responsible for the loan, both financially and physically, and, at his discretion, may require the borrower to insure the loan. He shall notify the Museum Committee immediately if a loan is not returned on time.

Copies of the forms for all outstanding loans shall be attached to the Collections Report at the end of the year.

The Curator shall be cautious about third-party loans, loans pending gift, long-term loans, loans for promotional purposes, and any loan differing from normal procedure.

DEACCESSIONING

In the event that an accessioned item is broken beyond repair, stolen beyond hope of recovery, or is surplus, the Curator shall notify the Board that he wishes it deaccessioned. If the Board approves, an entry shall be made in red ink against that object in the Accession Book and the catalogue cards shall be removed and placed in a dead file.

The number of items to be sold shall be held at a minimum and may be sold discreetly out of the geographic area. No item may be sold or traded if the donor is living. In the instance of donated items where the donor is deceased, the money received shall be used to buy other artifacts to be credited to that donor. No object deaccessioned from the collection may go to a member of the Board of Directors, a member of the Corporation, or the Curator.

EVALUATIONS

No member of the Board of Directors, no member of the Museum Committee, no member of the Society, nor the Curator, nor any employee or person holding a post of trust or honor in the _____ may give an evaluation on an object to a donor or prospective donor, nor may the Society nor any of these people pay for such an evaluation for tax purposes nor any other purpose. The Curator shall co-operate with donors who wish an evaluation and with their appraisers. The museum and the Society shall confine their activities in this area to the suggestion to donors of several knowledgeable appraisers. In the event that an accessioned item is insured or evaluated for identification purposes, this value may not be revealed to the donor.

OTHER PROVISIONS

Changes may be made to this manual from time to time on the advice of the Curator to the Museum Committee and with the approval of the Board.

In the event that the Society should adopt an ethics code, provision should be made for the Curator and other employees to buy and sell objects that might belong in the collection and to do this on their own behalf. The Curator or any other employee may not be in the business of buying and selling "antiques" or other collectible items, but may be allowed to evaluate collections for other museums and accept an honorarium for such purposes with the approval of the Board. No member of the Board who is in the business of buying and selling of "antiques" may sit on the Museum Committee.

The museum may not accept items on loan for repair, restoration, evaluation, or storage.

The Curator is expected to work with the Library Committee on the cataloguing of books in a manner suitable for libraries. He is expected to develop a suitable method of cataloguing and storage for historic photographs.

He is to establish a suitable method for the cataloguing of the archives.

Appendix C
Forms

This appendix contains several forms (listed below) that may be useful. Although you may not need them all, any of them can be adapted for individual use. All were originally designed to fit on an 8½-by-11-inch page, but in converting manuscript to typeset copy, some forms have been "telescoped" to fit. In setting them up for your own use, you may want to allow more space in areas where descriptions or detailed information is needed.

1. Example of a *Transfer-of-Title Form.*
2. Example of a page from an *Accession Register* for the One-Book Method.
3. Example of a page from the short form of the *Collections or Accessions Register.*
4. Example of a typed *Accession Sheet.*
5. Example of a simple printed *Accession Sheet.*
6. Example of a more complex printed *Accession Sheet.*
7. Example of a *Loan Form* for both loans *to and from* the museum.
8. Example of a *Loan Form* for a loan *to* the museum.
9. Example of a *Loan Form* for a loan *from* the museum.
10. Example of a *Catalogue Card.*
11. Example of an *Association Card.*
12. Example of a printed *Donor* or *Source Card.*
13. Example of a typed *Donor Card.*
14. Example of a *Photographic Record Card.*
15. Example of a *Receipt of Delivery Form.*
16. Example of a *Work Sheet* for inventory or as a register.
17. Example of a *Loan Register.*
18. Example of an *Acknowledgment of Gift Form.*

(C-1) Example of a *Transfer-of-Title Form*

HERO COUNTY HISTORICAL SOCIETY
Mansion on the Hill
Hero, Pennsylvania 15000

Gift Agreement

I, _____, hereby unconditionally give, donate, bestow and set over to the Hero County Historical Society, Hero, Pennsylvania, my property described on this sheet or on the reverse side of this sheet, to be used and/or disposed of by the Hero County Historical Society at its unrestricted discretion; and for myself, my distributees, and my personal representative, I waive all present or future rights in, to, or over said property, its use or disposition.

Signature_____ Date_____
Witness_____ Date_____

For the Hero County Historical Society _____

Title_____ Date_____

Description of Object(s):

[8 1/2"-X-11" paper]

(C-2) *Example of Page from Accession Register Using the One-Book Method*

Accession Number	Description	Source and Date
1	LEATHER KNIFE: Type used by shoemakers and leather workers to cut sheets of leather; shaped on the order of a food chopper, in a half-moon shape; has a flat wooden handle with a brass ferrule; has maker's name on blade but illegible. 5 ⅞" X 6 ⅝" overall.	B. Knott Forgotten Mausoleum Way Hero, Pa. 15000 2/6/72
2	GOUGE: Single piece, with integral handle; bezel on outside of handle; handle octagonal, stamped on one flat is "B. B. Specialty Co., Pittsburgh, Pa."; according to donor this was used to fit gun barrels to stocks; 11 ⅜"-long blade is 1" wide at cutting area.	Same
3	BREAD BASKET: Made of twisted ropes of grass woven into a basket by pieces of split wood (hickory?); bowl shaped; fair condition, as a piece of the rim is burned off; bottom has worn spots; 12 ¾" diameter X 4 ⅛", approximately; type used to make sourdough bread.	John O'Reilly Avaricious 810 Gelt Way Hero, Pa. 15000 4/8/72
4	CHAIR: Kitchen Windsor; has simple dished seat; bamboo design on posts and legs; tapered spindles; a single stretcher between each leg; painted red; at one time painted brown and then green; 32 ⅜" X 15 ⁹⁄₁₆" X 14 ¾" over-all.	Same
5	IBID.: Only 14 ⅜" wide.	Same
6	BOWL: Spatterware, soft clay; has white bezel; around rim is a blue-and-red design in a random pattern; in center of bowl is a tulip in red and green; excellent condition; a four-part mark is stamped on back; 8 ¾" diameter X 1 ¼" high.	Purchased from Raw Greed Antiques Gotcha Way Acme, Pa. 15100 for $75.00 5/10/72

[This example combines the Accession Register and the Accession Book all in one. The example here is using the One-Number System but could easily use the Two- or Three-Number System.]

(C-3) *Example of Page from an Accessions or Collections Register*

1967	Name of Donor	Accession	Date
67.1	Unknown	Unknown items found in collection	
67.2	Shem Ham	Grain shovel	1/3
67.3	Japheth Gomer	Tanner's Rake	1/3
67.4	Megog Medal	Painted Lectern	1/5
67.5	Javan Tubal	Cloth and clothing	1/6
67.6	Meshach Javan	Section of wooden waterpipe	1/6
67.7	Askenaz Ripath	Old Economy Co. brewing bottle	1/10
67.8	Togarmah Javan	1858 Mason jar	1/10
67.9	Elisha Tarshish	Bung-hole auger	1/10
67.10	Kittim Dodanim	2 Old Economy whiskey bottles	1/11
17.11	Ham Cush	Aaron Williams, *Harmony Society*	1/11
67.12	etc.		

[The purpose of the Accessions Register is to keep track of all the accessions in numerical order. In this example, only the accession number, the name of the donor, a short-form title, and the date accessioned are listed. In my opinion, this is all one really needs to know in this record. It is important to remember that the actual accession sheet is in another book.]

(C-4) *Example of a Typed Page from an Accession Book*

Donor: Mr. and Mrs. Lard Press
907 Sausage Avenue
Hero, Pa. 15000

February 26, 1976

76.3.1   *LEATHER KNIFE:* Type used by shoemakers and leather workers to cut sheets of leather; shaped on the order of a food chopper, in a half-moon shape; has a flat wooden handle with a brass ferrule; has maker's name on blade but illegible. 5 ⅞" X 6 ⅝" over-all.

76.3.2   *GOUGE:* Single piece, with integral handle; bezel on outside of handle; handle octagonal; stamped on one flat is "B. B. Speciality Co., Pittsburgh, Pa."; according to donor this was used to fit gun barrels to stocks; 11 ⅜"-long blade is 1"wide at cutting area.

76.3.3   *BREAD BASKET:* Made of twisted ropes of grass woven into a basket by pieces of split wood (hickory?); bowl-shaped; fair condition, as a piece of the rim is burned off; bottom has worn spots; 12 ¾" diameter X 4 ⅛", approximately; type used to make sourdough bread.

76.3.4   *CHAIR:* Kitchen Windsor; has simple dished seat; bamboo design on posts and legs; tapered spindles; a single stretcher between each leg; painted red; at one time painted brown and then green; 32 ⅜" X 15 ⁹⁄₁₆" X 14 ¾" over-all.

76.3.4   *IBID.:* Only 14 ⅜" wide.

76.3.6   *BOWL:* Spatterware, soft clay; has white bezel; around rim is a blue-and-red design in a random pattern; in center of bowl is a tulip in red and green; excellent condition; a four-part mark is stamped on back; 8 ¾" diameter X 1 ¼" high.

[You might notice that this is almost the same as the Accession Register page in C-2. The difference is only one of degree. The page in the Accession Register in C-2 has both the Register and the Accession Sheet on one page. In the more complex systems, these two elements are separated. (C-3 and C-4). The Accession Sheet fits into an Accession Book. It may be either hand-written or typed. It must be accompanied by a separate Accession Register (such as C-3).]

(C-5) *Example of a Simple Printed Accession Sheet*

Hero County Historical Society
Mansion on the Hill
Hero, Pennsylvania 15000

ACCESSION SHEET

Source: Date:

Gift Agrmnt.   [ ]
Donor Ackn.   [ ]
Cat. Card   [ ]
Donor Card   [ ]
Assoc. Card   [ ]
Photo.   [ ]
Neg. No. _____

Gift [ ]   Purchase [ ]   Source of Funds _____

Accession Number	Description

(C-6) *Example of a More Complex Printed Accession Sheet*

Hero County Historical Society
Mansion on the Hill
Hero, Pennsylvania 15000

ACCESSION SHEET

Source: Date:

Gift Agrmnt.	[ ]
Donor Card	[ ]
Donor Ackn.	[ ]
Newsletter	[ ]
Cat. Card	[ ]
Assoc. Card	[ ]
Photo.	[ ]
Neg. No.	_____

Gift [ ]   Purchase [ ]   Source of Funds _____
Association:

Accession Number	Item	Description

[If you insure your collection or wish to evaluate individual objects in the collection, you may wish to add a fourth column on the right for an evaluation. Figures should be entered in pencil. You may wish to leave out the vertical columns.]

(C-7) *Example of a Single Loan Form for Both Types of Loan*

HERO COUNTY HISTORICAL SOCIETY
Mansion on the Hill
Hero, Pennsylvania 15000

Lent to_____   Address _____
Lent from_____   Address _____
Purpose _____   Insurance by_____
Date from_____   Date to_____
Transportation by_____   Date of form_____
How valued_____   Total value_____

The Hero County Historical Society agrees to borrow/lend from/to _____ (the second party) the below-listed items for the purpose(s) and date(s) given. The lender states that the item(s) in this loan are his property. No item may be used for other purposes or lent to a third party without the agreement of the owner. The borrower agrees to treat the objects in this loan as his own under the agreement of the owner. All changes in this agreement must be in writing with the consent of both parties. The Hero County Historical Society does not accept any condition(s) unless set forth in this form.

(Note Condition)

For Hero County Historical Society_____Date_____
For second party_____Date_____
If second party is not owner, state authority_____
Return:
Received by_____from_____
If person receiving item(s) is not owner, state authority____
Date _____
Condition on return if other than above_____

Page_____of_____

(C-8) *Example of a Loan Form for a Loan to the Museum*

LOAN TO

The Hero County Historical Museum

Mansion on the Hill
Hero, Pennsylvania 15000
(444) 266-4500

Name _____ Date _____

Address_____

_____ Zip_____

If an organization, the name and title of the authorizing official:
Name_____Title_____
Telephone number(s) (   )_____
Dates of loan wall to wall, from_____to_____
Who transports? _____How? _____

Lends the below-listed object(s) to the Hero County Historical Society under the conditions set forth on the back of this form. All pages of the loan form must be signed by both parties. If there are other conditions of the loan, they must be listed on this form.

For the Hero County Historical Society   For the Lender
Signature_____   Signature _____
Title _____   Title _____
Date _____   Date _____

_____
_____

Release:
  Received in the condition   noted
  Name_____ Date_____

  Released for the Museum by
  Name_____ Title_____

_____

Loan No.   Object   Value

_____

[If necessary, the subsequent sheets of this form can be blank sheets of paper. If the museum does not use loan numbers, that may be omitted. It is not necessary to use all of the conditions on the reverse of this form.]

Reverse Side of Loan Form

CONDITIONS OF LOANS TO THE HERO COUNTY HISTORICAL SOCIETY

1. The Hero County Historical Society agrees to treat the object(s) lent to the museum as if they were the property of the museum.

2. The Society agrees to use the object(s) only in the manner and for the purpose set forth in this form and will not lend to a third party unless agreed upon.

3. The condition of the object(s) is as noted on this form.

4. In the event of damage or loss, the Society agrees to compensate the lender up to the value of the object as noted on the form through its insurance company.

5. If the lender elects to maintain his own insurance during the loan, he must furnish the Society with proof of insurance.

6. Unless the Society agrees to move the object, it will not be responsible for the costs of moving. If the lender terminates the loan before the agreed time, the lender will be responsible for moving the object from the museum.

7. This loan may not be for more than one year from delivery of the object(s). In the event that the loan is extended, a new loan form must be agreed upon and signed by both parties.

8. The Society agrees to place a notice in some public form on or near the object acknowledging the loan.

9. The Society will surrender the object to the lender only upon the lender's signing this form and indicating that the loan has been returned. If the lender dies, or can not receive the loan personally, the estate, or the third party must have proof of their authority to receive the loan.

10. The loan is for the dates indicated. In the event that the lender does not pick up his property, or cannot receive it, the museum maintains the right of disposing of the object(s) or charging a storage fee ninety (90) days after the termination date. A registered letter is considered an adequate notice of the museum's attempt to notify the lender of their attempt to return the loan.

11. This agreement may be amended by the agreement of both parties at any time during the loan.

(C-9) *Example of a Loan Form for Loans from a Museum*

LOAN FROM

The Hero County Historical Society
Mansion on the Hill
Hero, Pennsylvania 15000
(444) 728-2208

Date _____

Date _____

Name_____
Address_____
_____Zip _____
If an organization, name and title of responsible person:
Name_____Title_____
Date of loan, wall to wall, from_____to_____
Purpose of loan_____
Location during loan_____
Total value of loan_____How valued?_____
Who transports loan?_____How?_____
Is a third party involved?_____

Accession No.	Description	Condition	Value

[A blank sheet of paper may be used for subsequent pages.]

For the Hero County Historical
Society:

Returned: Date_____   _____Title_____
                                     Date Signed _____
For Society _____   The Borrower:
For Borrower _____   _____Title_____
                                     Date Signed _____

If more than one page, both parties must sign all pages. Note special conditions, acknowledgments, etc., on loan form. Conditions of the loan are given on the back of this form.

Reverse Side of "Loan From" Form

CONDITIONS OF LOANS FROM THE MUSEUM

1. It is understood that the objects in this loan will remain in the condition received and will not be repaired, restored, cleaned, or altered in any way without the permission of the museum. The condition is understood to be as stated on the form.

2. All damages to objects at any point in this loan from wall to wall will be reported to the museum immediately.

3. The object(s) may not be lent to a third party without the advance approval of the museum.

4. The object(s) may be photographed only with the permission of the museum. The borrower agrees that the photographs taken of this loan will be used only for the purpose stated on this form and only for the number of times stated. The museum will receive a copy of all photographs for record purposes. All publications of photographs of items in this loan will bear a credit line acknowledging that the object is the property of the Hero County Historical Museum.

5. The borrower is responsible for packing, transportation, insurance, and all other factors of transporting the loan, unless otherwise stated. The borrower is responsible for returning the loan at the time stated.

6. The museum may require proof of insurance, may wish to have its name on the policy, and may wish to receive a copy of the insurance policy.

7. The borrower agrees to use the loan only for the purposes stated on this form.

(C-10) Example of a Catalogue Card

Acc. No.	Object: Source: Loc.: Date: Association: Size: Material:

HERO COUNTY HISTORICAL SOCIETY

[The description is written in the blank very much in the manner that it appears on the accession sheet. "Loc." stands for the location of the object and should be written in pencil. "Date" refers to date of manufacture or creation. If such things as provenance, country or place of origin, and the like are important, they can be added easily. The reason that the name of the museum is written at the bottom is that you will need to identify your cards, but the most important information on the card is the accession number and the name of the object, and that should be at the top where it can be seen easily.]

(C-11) *Example of an Association Card*

```
┌─────────────────────────────────────────────────────────┐
│ ASSOCIATION                                              │
│                                                          │
│ Name:                                                    │
│ Location:                                                │
│ Date(s): _____ to _____           │
│ Other information:                                       │
│                                                          │
├─────────────────────────────────────────────────────────┤
│ Accession number(s):        Object:                      │
│                                                          │
│                                                          │
│                                                          │
│                                                          │
│                                                          │
│                                                          │
│              HERO COUNTY HISTORICAL MUSEUM               │
└─────────────────────────────────────────────────────────┘
```

[The name of the association might be a person, a place, an event, or even an object. The location is the place most closely related to the Association. Dates would be the time the Association existed. Other information might be a quick background on the Association. The accession numbers refer to the museum's accessions that have this association. An even simpler version of this card appears in the text.]

(C-12) *Example of a Printed Donor or Source Card*

Donor or Source:
        Address:

Association, If any:

Accession numbers:

                    HERO COUNTY HISTORICAL MUSEUM

[As pointed out in the text, it is about as easy to type this information on a blank card. If the source is associated with an event, an office, or an important family, it is a good idea to list that on the Donor Card. It is a good idea to have a card for both the donor and the source of a purchase.]

(C-13) *Example of a Typed Donor Card*

```
B. Knott Forgotten
Mausoleum Way
Hero, PA 15000



1-2
468-72
968
1002
```

[A number of museums like to put the name of the object by each accession number on a donor card. This is very handy, but it can be rather clumsy in the case of large accessions. What you would be doing is creating another catalogue card. The Donor Card is meant only as a reference and should be kept simple.]

(C-14) *Example of a Photographic Record Card*

Acc. No.	Object:
Neg. No.	Source:

Description:

HERO COUNTY HISTORICAL MUSEUM

[On this card I have placed only a contact from a 35mm black-and-white negative. A larger format may be used. The description may be redundant with the photograph and the fact that there is a catalogue card, too. The easiest way to have a photographic record is to glue the print to a catalogue card. Samples of more ambitious photographic catalogue cards can be seen in Graham or Dudley and Wilkinson.]

(C-15) *An example of a Receipt of Delivery Form*

RECEIPT OF DELIVERY TO
The Hero County Historical Society
Mansion on the Hill
Hero, Pennsylvania 15000
(444) 266-4500

This is to acknowledge receipt of the below-listed items by the Hero County Historical Society from

Name _____Date _____
Address_____
_____ Zip _____
Telephone number(s)_____
From _____to _____

The Society will agree to hold this loan only for the dates indicated. The lender is responsible for pick-up and delivery. Condition is as indicated.

For the Society: The Lender:
Signature _____   Signature _____
Title _____   Title _____

Item and Description

[This form is used for a variety of purposes. Its usual purpose is to hold potential accessions until they can be examined by a competent person. Another use is to hold accessions or loans until the proper forms can be filled out. If the objects are accepted, the museum will be required to get a Gift Agreement signed. Other uses are for the return of loans, the delivery of nonaccessionable items to the museum, and as a receipt. Some museums add the clause that they are not responsible for items left under these agreements, but, as I have pointed out, the museum is usually responsible. A small museum will probably find this form unnecessary.]

(Page of)

Release:

Received from the Hero County Historical Society, the above-listed items.
Signature _____Date _____

(C-16) Work Sheet for
Inventories or Registers

[With this form, you can inventory any number of objects by adding hundreds or thousands in front of the digit.]

No.   *Object*

0.
1.
2.
3.
4.
5.

6.
7.
8.
9.
10.

11.
12.
13.
14.
15.

16.
17.
18.
19.
20.

21.
22.
23.
24.
25.

26.
27.
28.
29.
30.

31.
32.
33.
34.
35.

36.
37.
38.
39.
40.

41.
42.
43.
44.
45.

46.
47.
48.
49.

Work Sheet for
Inventories or Registers

No.   Object

50.
51.
52.
53.
54.
55.
_____
56.
57.
58.
59.
60.
_____
61.
62.
63.
64.
65.
_____
66.
67.
68.
69.
70.
_____
71.
72.
73.
74.
75.
_____
76.
77.
78.
79.
80.
_____
81.
82.
83.
84.
85.
_____
86.
87.
88.
89.
90.
_____
91.
92.
93.
94.
95.
_____
96.
97.
98.
99.
_____

(C-17) Example of a Loan Register

Loan No.	Source	Object	Description	Dates from/to	Condition	Insurance	Returned

[Some museums register only incoming loans, and some register both incoming and outgoing loans. Unless you lend out a great number, I suggest using this form for only incoming loans. The purpose of the loan number is to place a temporary number on the loan, so all objects in the museum will have a number.]

(C-18) *Example of a Printed Acknowledgment-of-Gift Form*

THE BOARD OF TRUSTEES
of
THE HERO COUNTY HISTORICAL SOCIETY
Gratefully Acknowledge
Your Gift
to
THE MUSEUM

_____

President, Board of Trustees

[These are generally engraved or well printed on fine card stock. There is often room at the bottom to acknowledge exactly what it was that was given to the museum. I prefer a personal letter, but circumstances may dictate that this form, in either card or letter form, is what the museum will use to acknowledge gifts. It is best to have it very well printed.]

Appendix D

(D-1) *Example of Annual Report by a Curator or Collections Committee*

ANNUAL REPORT OF THE COLLECTIONS COMMITTEE OF THE HERO COUNTY HISTORICAL SOCIETY FOR THE YEAR 1979.

In the year 1979, we had 46 accessions, totalling 408 items. One of the most outstanding gifts during the year was the one-wheeled automobile, called the "Gyrogo," given to us by the estate of Vary Eccentric. Another outstanding gift was the portrait of John Hero, founder of the town, given by Mr. and Mrs. John C. Hero VI. A list of accessions is attached.

We have only one outstanding loan to the museum. This is the lard press in the "Made in Hero" exhibit, to be returned in March 1980. The only other loans to the museum were 26 quilts from 22 Society members for the quilt show. All but one of these has been returned. The remaining quilt was given to us by the owner, Mrs. George Needlecase, at the conclusion of the show. We have one outstanding loan from the museum and this is the 1876 isometric view of Hero that has been lent to the State Museum for its exhibit of town views. This will be returned in October 1980.

We cleaned the textile storage areas and audited the catalogue of the textiles and costumes before the quilt show. We found enough discrepancies that we had to recatalogue the whole textile collection. For this task, we had the services of the Hero Hand Weavers' Guild. We also washed and stored all the glassware.

We spent a great deal of time straightening our storage and cleaning the items on exhibit. We believe that the condition of the collection is good and greatly improved over last year.

We do not recommend that any object in the collection be deaccessioned this year.

Respectfully submitted,
I. M. Acquisitive, Chairman
Collections Committee

[The supporting documents have been omitted.]

(D-2) *Qualifying Clause for Register's Manual*

The curator will assemble all the records of the Society related to the collection and try to justify them with the collection. It is recognized that a reasonably adequate system of registration was used for this portion of the collection but that it was not completely or consistently applied. The curator will correct as many errors as he can and bring the old registration system up to the standards of this manual. All outstanding loans will be cleared as soon as possible.

All objects that exist in the collection at the time this manual is adopted (_____) and that do not have any apparent records will be considered a single accession and will be assigned one accession number, preferably the first number issued under the new system.

Objects that do have numbers and/or are related to the records will keep the accession numbers they have and discrepancies will be removed as well as possible.

When the existing collection has been completely audited, the curator will write a report on what he has done, giving the exact steps; and this will be filed with the collections report at the next annual meeting.

[This clause may be added to the registrar's manual in Appendix B if there is an existing collection in the museum and the museum is not satisfied with its registration. I cannot write a clause that will fit every circumstance, and this one is meant only as a guideline.]

(D-3) *Items Needed to Accession and Catalogue*

#2 Pencils
Paper tags
3"-x-5" file drawer for lexicon[1]
4"-x-6" file for catalogue cards
4"-x-6" cards[2]
1/2 pint of sign-painters' enamel, red[3]
1/2 pint of sign-painters' enamel, white
#000 or #0000 lettering brushes
Bottle of high-quality clear nail polish
Fine crow-quill pen
Textile-marking pen (laundry pen)[4]
India ink, black
Record book(s) with inert paper and/or 8 1/2"-x-11" acid-free typing paper
Bottle of turpentine (to clean brushes)
Bottle of nail-polish remover

1. The "cards" used in the lexicon should be of ordinary writing paper cut to size. This takes less room than bulkier note cards.

2. It is difficult to find a source of supply for 4"-x-6"catalogue cards made of inert paper and already cut. They usually have to be ordered cut. However, 3"-x-5" cards on inert paper are readily available.

3. Sign-painters' enamel is usually available at art supply stores. If such a store is not available, a high-quality oil-base glossy enamel can be used.

4. These are available at almost any five-and-ten or drug store.

Bibliographical Note

What amazed me when I set out to write this book was how little has actually been published about museum registration. I had thought there would be quite a bit. Most of what is written repeats that you put down the year of accession first, then the number of the accession, and then the number of the object, and then you have a number, such as 69.22.—and that is what registration is all about.

If there were only one book on museum registration, that book would be Dorothy H. Dudley and Irma Bexold Wilkinson et al., *Museum Registration Methods,* revised edition (Washington, D.C.: American Association of Museums, 1968). It has the shortcomings, so far as small historical agencies are concerned, discussed in the preface of *this* book, but all in all, it is *The* book. A second revised edition is forthcoming and should appear about the middle of 1978. In many respects, the 1958 edition is much better for small historical museums than the 1968. (Hereafter, the American Association of Museums is referred to as "AAM.")

Although it is somewhat overwhelming, I like "A Method of Museum Registration," by John M. Graham II, *Museum News,* 42, no. 8 (April 1965), which has been issued several times by AAM as a technical leaflet (number 2) and is still in print. If we could have a dream system, this would be it.

The rest of the literature is listed in alphabetical order.

George Bowditch, "Cataloguing Photographs: A Procedure for Small Museums," *Technical Leaflet #57,* revised (Nashville: American Association for State and Local History, 1975). Bowditch's system is much better than mine, but it is more time-consuming. Hereafter, the American Association for State and Local History will be referred to as "AASLH."

Stephan F. Borhegyi and Alice Marriott, "Proposals for a Standardized Museum Accessioning and Classification System," *Curator,* 1:2 (1958). I heard Borhegyi deliver this as an address. It is mainly for anthropology museums, but it is too bad the idea was never carried further.

The shape of things to come can be seen in two books by Robert G. Chenhall, *Museum Cataloguing in the Computer Age* (Nashville:

AASLH, 1978) and *Nomenclature for Museum Cataloguing*, also published by AASLH (1975). I was able to read the latter only in proof. Chenhall is certainly a great thinker, and his will be the ideas that will be adopted in the future. The computer may force a standardization on the museum field, which is something that no human being will ever be able to do.

Janson L. Cox., "Photographing Historical Collections: Equipment, Methods and Bibliography," *Technical Leaflet #63* (Nashville: AASLH, 1973).

The system I was trained under is set forth in the Detroit Historical Museum, *Registrar's Manual*, revised edition (Detroit: DHM, 1973). Although I have long since parted from many of its ways, it is a good model to follow. If you want to see a system a little bit more complex than I have set forth in appendix B, then you might write to them and ask them for a copy: Detroit Hitorical Museum, 5401 Woodward, Detroit, Michigan 48202. It is the system that Guthe (q.v.) adapted in his works and the one used for historical museums in Dudley and Wilkinson (q.v.). Most of the material in it was written by Margo Pearsall. Until my institution adopted its own registrar's manual, I used this one.

Walter S. Dunn, Jr., "Cataloguing Ephemera: A Procedure for Small Libraries," AASLH *Technical Leaflet #58*(1972).

Thomas E. Felt, *Researching, Writing, and Publishing Local History* (Nashville: AASLH, 1976) is aimed at publications, but the techniques are the same for collections.

Carl E. Guthe was one of the great thinkers of the museum field and his books were about the first technical literature (except, perhaps, for Coleman) that were circulated popularly. Although more than twenty years have gone by since he wrote his *So You Want A Good Museum?* revised edition (Washington, D.C: AAM, 1967), It is still well worth reading, and many of the things he says still hold true. Written in the same vein, but with more emphasis on historical agencies, is his *The Management of Small Historical Museums*, second edition (Nashville: AASLH, 1969). His "Documenting Collections: Museum Registration and Records," AASLH *Technical Leaflet #11* (1963), is very useful, but in it, to my mind, documentation and registration seem too closely intermingled.

Eugene Kramer, "Collecting Historical Artifacts: An Aid for Small Museums," AASLH *Technical Leaflet #6* (1970).

David Kaser, "The Library in the Small Historical Society," *AASLH Technical Leaflet #27*, revised (1972).

Basic Museums Management by, George McBeth and S. James

Gooding (Ottawa: Canadian Museum Association, 1969) has a succinct chapter on registration. The book is the text for a mail-order museum course, and supplemental material that is quite useful was available from the Canadian Museums Association.

Anita Manning, "Converting Loans to Gifts: One Solution to 'Permanent' Loans," AASLH *Technical Leaflet #94* (1977), is a very practical solution to a severe problem. Reading this leaflet is enough to prevent new museums from ever making a "permanent" loan.

Frederick L. Rathe, Jr., and Merrilyn Rogers O'Connell, *Guide to Historical Preservation, Historical Agencies, and Museum Practices* (Cooperstown: New York State Historical Association, 1970) is rapidly being replaced by *A Bibliogaphy on Historical Organization Practices,* a new series of bibliographies edited by the same team and published by AASLH, Since the volume that will contain the bibliography on registration practices has not yet been issued, however, this older edition will prove useful in all museum practices.

In 1967, I was an angry young man and wrote an angry article that amazes me when I read it now, but in it I first raised the question "Why *have* the huge registration apparatus for small museums?" This was Daniel B Reibel, "The Challenge of the Future of History Museums," *Curator*, X, no. 3 (1967): 253-260. I first proposed a simple system in "Cataloguing Your Collection," *The Chronicle of the Early American Industries Association*, 27, no. 3 (September 1974): 53-55. This book is an outgrowth of that article.

Paul Vanderbilt, "Filing Your Photographs: Some Basic Procedures," *AASLH Technical Leaflet #36* (1966).

Collection, Use, and Care of Historic Photographs by Robert A. Weinstein and Larry Booth, Nashville: AASLH, (1977) refers only to historic photographs, and they propose a much better system than I do, but, again, it is more time-consuming. If the small museum has a large collection of historic photographs, it would do well to look at this book.

Mary Theime's slide/tape production on registration, *Registration of Museum Objects*, Slide Tape Training Kit #4 (Nashville: AASLH 1974), with its seventy-eight slides plus tape, gives a rationale for a registration system and shows the step-by-step registration of an object. The system demonstrated is somewhat more complex than the one in this book. Ms. Thieme uses a subject catalogue that is a little more complex than the association catalogue in this book, but it is worth considering. She also has a receipt and a deposit receipt, which may be an excessive number of forms, but she does show how the latter is used. Use of slide/tapes is a good training device for volunteers, no matter what system you use.

There is a registrar's journal, *Registrar's Report,* issued quarterly. The first issue (May 1977) raised the question of just what the role of the registrar is. Write to P.O. Box 112, Bicentennial Station, Los Angeles, California 90048. At the AAM meeting, which is held in the spring, a registrar's section meets and has its own organization. Many large museums print their registrars' manuals and are happy to share them. Also, do not forget related library material, especially that on cataloguing.

Index